Natural Harvest

An inspirational collection of semen-based recipes

by Paul "Fotie" Photenhauer

CookingWithCum.com

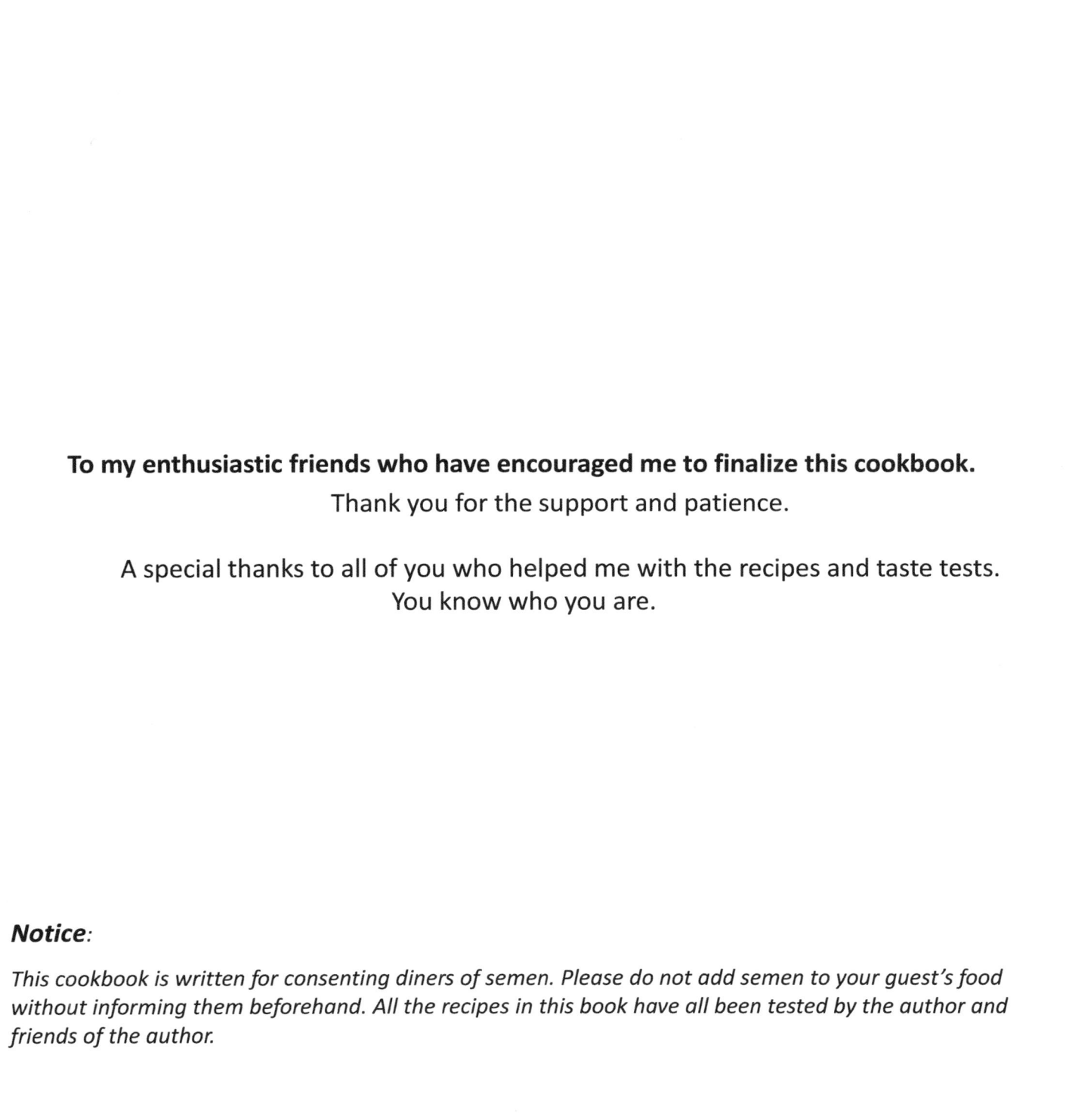

To my enthusiastic friends who have encouraged me to finalize this cookbook.
Thank you for the support and patience.

A special thanks to all of you who helped me with the recipes and taste tests.
You know who you are.

Notice*:*

This cookbook is written for consenting diners of semen. Please do not add semen to your guest's food without informing them beforehand. All the recipes in this book have all been tested by the author and friends of the author.

INTRODUCTION

We humans are truly omnivores – we will eat just about anything. As long as something edible either tastes good, makes us feel good, provides energy, nutrition, or adds a pleasurable texture we find ways to eat it. Anyone who has travelled abroad knows that foods we might find strange or unpleasant may be considered delicacies in other countries. Rotten fish is a national dish in Sweden, while Australians spread concentrated yeast extract on their breakfast toast. The British love their blood sausage, and guinea pigs are roasted for dinner in Peru. All the while, Americans and Europeans consume vast amounts of milk and other dairy products that consist of mammary secretions from cows. Compared to semen, milk might be considered positively disgusting.

Semen is not only nutritious, but it also has a palatable texture and wonderful cooking properties. Like fine wine and cheeses, the taste of semen is complex and dynamic. Semen producers can generate a wide range of semen tastes simply by making minor dietary adjustments. Semen is inexpensive to produce and is commonly available in many, if not most, homes and restaurants. Despite all of these positive qualities, semen remains neglected as a food. This book hopes to change that.

Once you overcome any initial hesitation, you will be surprised to learn how wonderful semen is in the kitchen. Semen is an exciting ingredient that can give every dish you make an interesting twist. If you, like us, are a passionate cook and are not afraid to experiment with new ingredients - you will love this cookbook.

Fotie

Drinks

Semen adds an exciting personal touch to your favorite cocktail. Semen and alcohol are a great combination because alcohol actually enhances the delicate semen flavors. Semen is easily added to any beverage that uses milk or cream.

- High Protein Smoothie - Page 10
- Almost White Russian - Page 11
- Strawberry Splasharita - Page 12
- Irish coffee with Extra Cream - Page 13
- Cappuccino di seme - Page 15

Appetizers

Seafood and semen are made for each other. Adding semen to common appetizers is a great way to get the conversation started at your next dinner party. Semen will surely become the main attraction and may even steal the show.

- Slightly Saltier Caviar - Page 16
- Moules Marinières de L'homme - Page 18
- Man Made Oysters - Page 20
- Glazed Grilled Pink Salmon - Page 23

Chef's note: Try the man-made oysters for a daring gastronomic example of semen as food.

Main Courses

Many main meals - especially meat dishes - are too heavy to allow the nuanced properties of semen to be properly enjoyed. The joy derived from dining on these dishes comes primarily from knowing that the semen is in there.

> Tuna Sashimi with Homemade Dipping Sauce - Page 24
>
> Roasted Lamb with Good Gravy - Page 27
>
> Veal Scaloppini - Page 29
>
> Noodles with Special Spicy Sauce - Page 31
>
> Lumpier Lumpia - Page 33
>
> Chicken Noodle Soup - Page 35

Chef's note: It may come as a surprise to find a recipe for Lumpia in this cookbook. The reason I included this exotic and delectable recipe is that Filipino friend of ours passionately insisted on contributing this very special recipe.

Sauces

Semen can make any sauce more exciting. The sauces should be of the "full fat" variety so don't even think about calories when making these sauces.

      Special "S" BBQ Sauce - Page 36

      Hollandaise Sauce - Page 38

      Pungent Aioli - Page 41

Desserts

A good dessert is the climax of any meal. For maximum freshness and the greatest visual appeal, add the semen right before serving. If the dining situation allows for more intimacy, you may wish to add the semen at the table which makes for a truly memorable dessert.

Creamy Cum Crêpes - Page 43

Cum Crème Caramel - Page 44

Cream Éclair - Page 47

Spunky Candied Pecans - Page 48

Creamy Dessert - Panna Cotta - Page 50

Chocolate Truffles with White Center - Page 53

Tiramisu Surprise - Page 54

Chef's note: Desserts are a great place to start if you are new to cooking with semen.

High Protein Smoothie

Unlike other high protein drinks this one does not use animal proteins such as eggs or whey for nutrition.

1 Cup Diced Kiwi

1 Ripe Banana

1 Cup of Soy Milk

1-3 Tablespoons of Fresh Semen

Ice Cubes

Throw everything into a blender and liquify.

Chef's Note: *This is a great drink to experiment with. Try substituting peaches or strawberries for the kiwi.*

Almost White Russian

This cocktail was re-vitalized by 'Dude' in the film 'The Big Lebowski'

2 Oz. Vodka

1 Oz. Coffee Liqueur

½ Oz. Semen

Cream or Milk

Ice Cubes

Pour vodka, semen and coffee liqueur over ice cubes and top up the glass with milk or cream.

Strawberry Splasharita

1 Cup Frozen Sliced Strawberries

1/2 Cup Good-Quality Tequila

1/4 Cup Triple Sec

1 Tablespoon Fresh Semen

2 Cups Crushed Ice

Combine all ingredients except semen in a blender and blend until smooth. Pour into a sugar-rimmed glass.

Float the semen over the drink. It will coagulate as it cools and adds a splendid finishing touch to this popular drink.

IRISH COFFEE WITH EXTRA CREAM

1-2 Shots of Whisky

2 Teaspoon Brown Sugar

Hot Freshly Brewed Coffee, Or a Double Shot Of

Espresso

Lightly Whipped Cream

1 Tablespoon Semen

If using freshly ejaculated semen let it melt before continuing. Dissolve the brown sugar and semen into the whisky in a glass. The semen sometimes takes some stirring to dissolve completely, but it is worth the effort since semen lumps are not a stylish addition to this soothing drink.

Add the coffee up to ½ inch from the rim of the glass. Carefully add the lightly whipped cream on top.

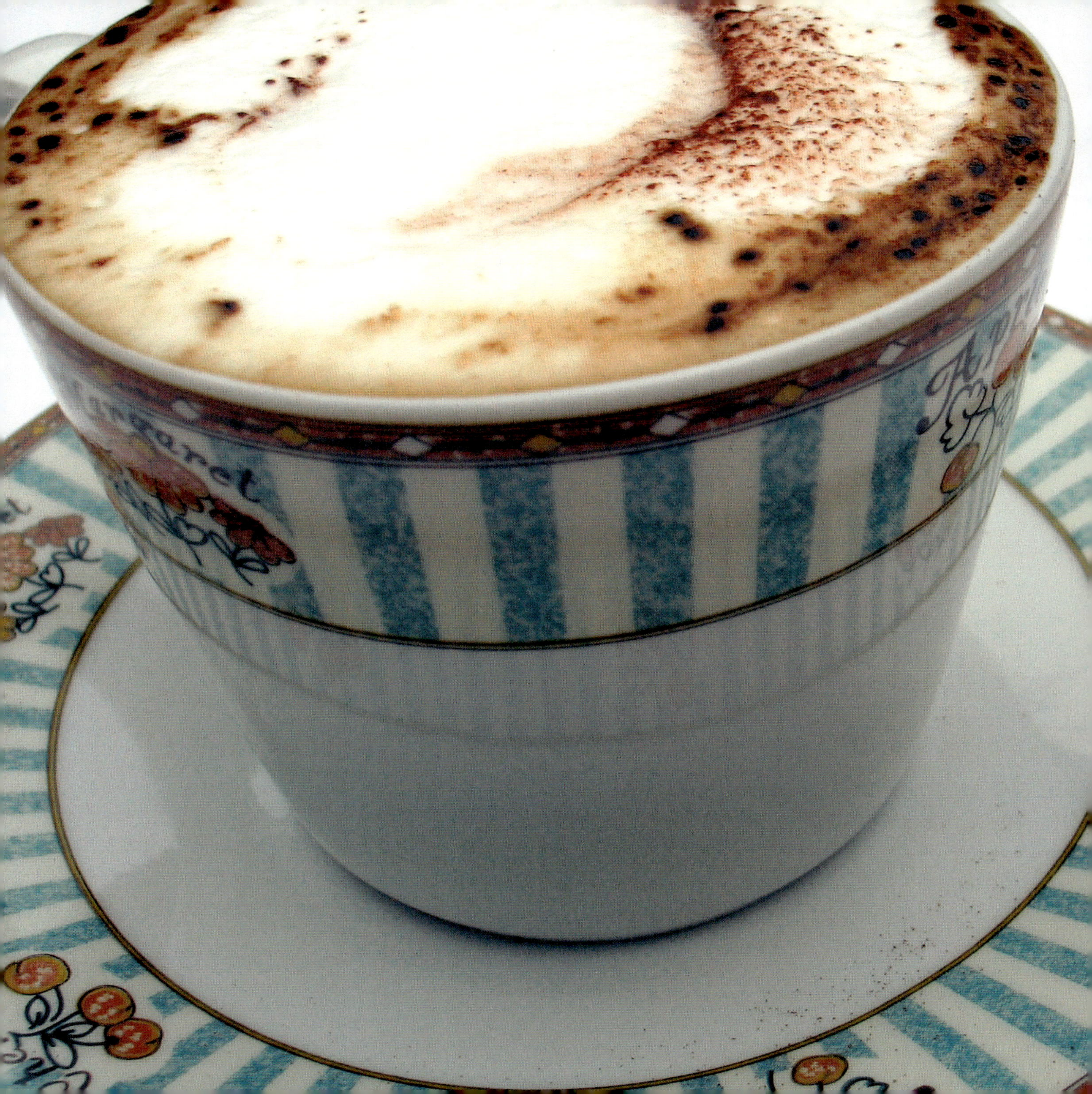

Cappuccino Di seme

This smooth creamy coffee drink makes good use of the frothing qualities of semen. In Italy a cappuccino is usually served for breakfast, and since semen quality and volume is often excellent after a good night's sleep - this is a perfect way to begin the day.

Making a good cappuccino takes some practice but the recipe is simple: one shot of quality espresso, some steamed milk, and a shot of semen. Mixing the semen with the milk before steaming enhances the flavors of both the milk and the semen. If you do not have a milk steamer then you can heat the mixture in a saucepan while whisking continuously.

SLIGHTLY SALTIER CAVIAR

Like semen, caviar is often considered an acquired taste. If you have not yet learned to appreciate caviar on its own, this decadent combination of semen and caviar will leave your mouth begging for more.

1 3/4 Oz. (50g) Tin of the Finest Caviar You Can Afford

1 Tablespoon of Fresh Semen

Simply open the tin of caviar and very gently (so that the eggs don't break) stir in the semen.

Caviar should be spooned carefully on lightly toasted bread or directly into the mouth. When serving and eating caviar, avoid using utensils made of silver because this will impart a metallic taste. Serve on ice for maximum freshness.

Use only a high-grade caviar and high quality semen. Serve the dish pure, without any lemon or garnishes like chopped egg, onion or sour cream.

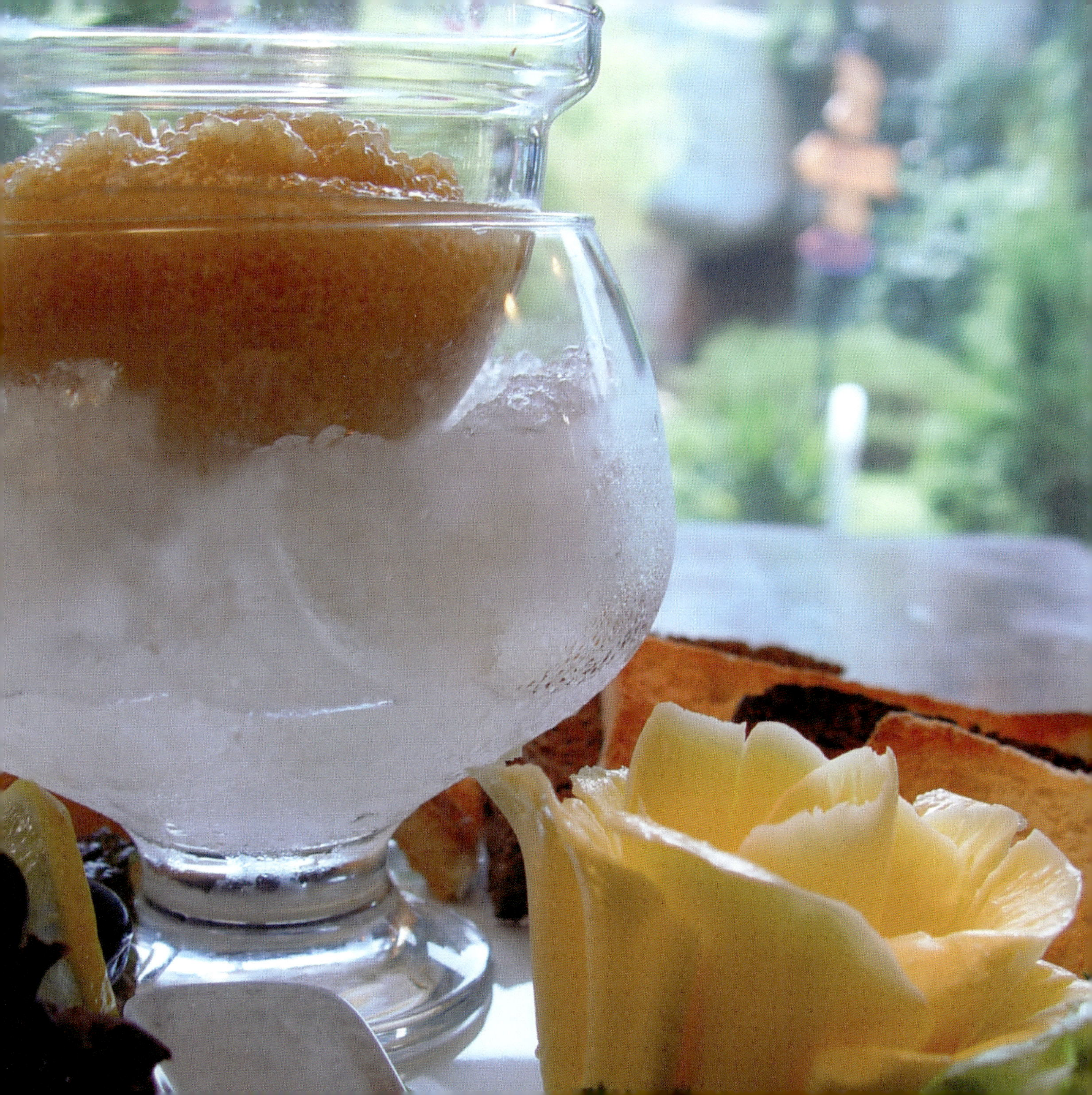

Moules Mariniere de l'homme

Fresh mussels steamed in white wine and served in their own and your own sauce combined. What could possibly be better? In France the mussels are served with fries and a dry cider.

½ lb. – 1 lb. Live Mussels

1/2 Cup Dry White Wine

1/4 Cup Chopped Shallots

1-2 Cloves Minced Garlic

1 Tablespoon Chopped Parsley

4 Tablespoons Butter

1 Tablespoon Semen

Scrub and debeard the mussels, removing any that are open or otherwise damaged. Melt butter in a large sauce pan and whisk in the semen.

Sauté the shallots and herbs in a large saucepan over medium heat before increasing heat to high and adding the mussels and wine.

Steam 5-6 minutes until shells open.

Discard any unopened shells and serve immediately with the semen-mussel nectar poured over the mussels.

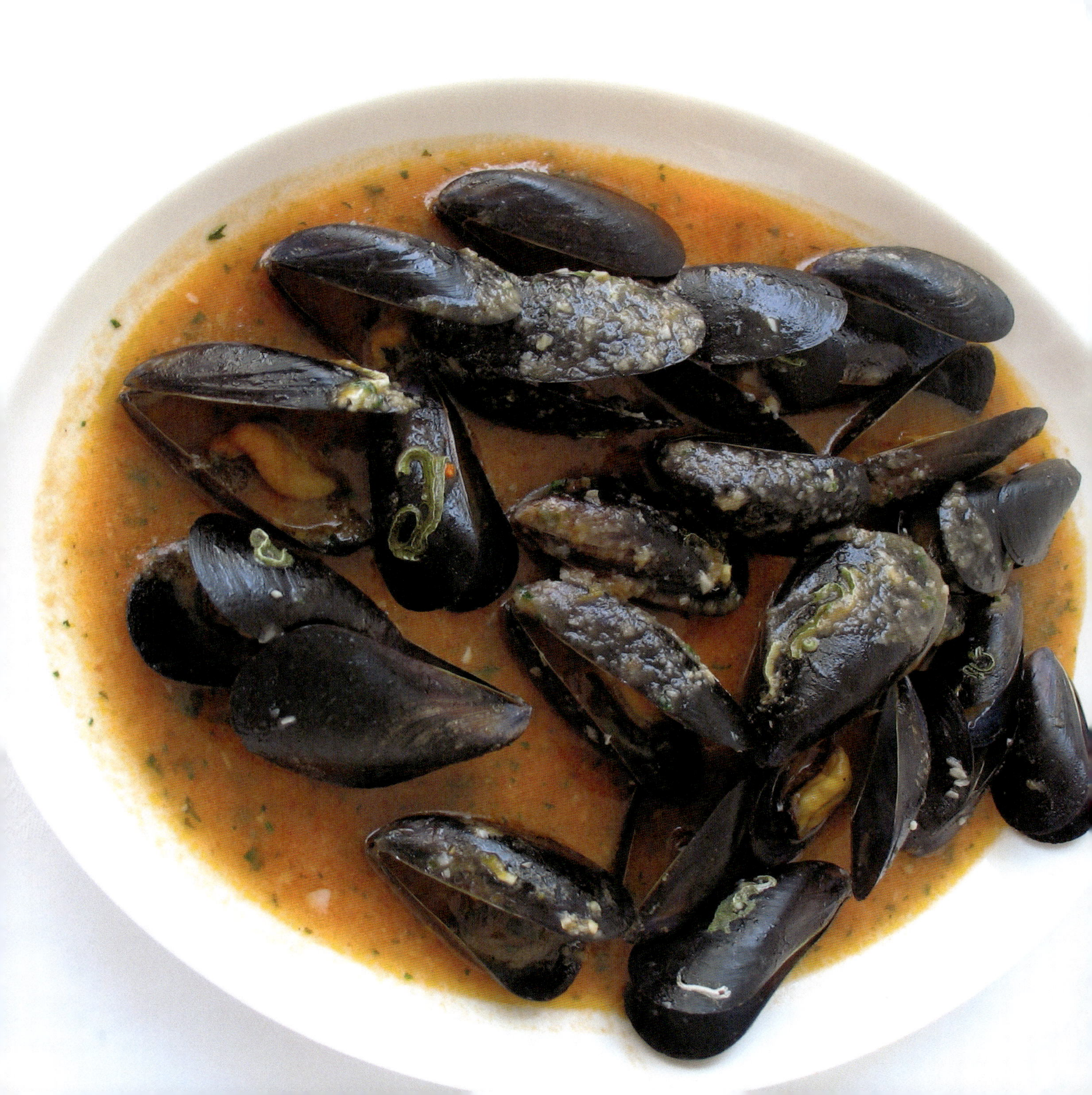

Man-Made Oysters

Oysters are so beautiful, it is a shame to throw away the shells after just one meal. Re-savor the feeling of a silky succulent oyster slipping down your throat by using the shells as semen serving dishes.

Cleaned Oyster Shells

Chilled Fresh Semen, the More the Better

Ice

Lemon and Pepper Garnish

First clean the oyster shells in cold water. Do not use soap since the shell easily absorbs the nasty taste of soap. Spoon the chilled fresh semen into each shell. Serve simply on ice with just a squeeze of fresh lemon and maybe a grind of black pepper.

Chef's note: *A true semen connoisseur might forego the lemon and pepper in favor of the non-adulterated semen flavor.*

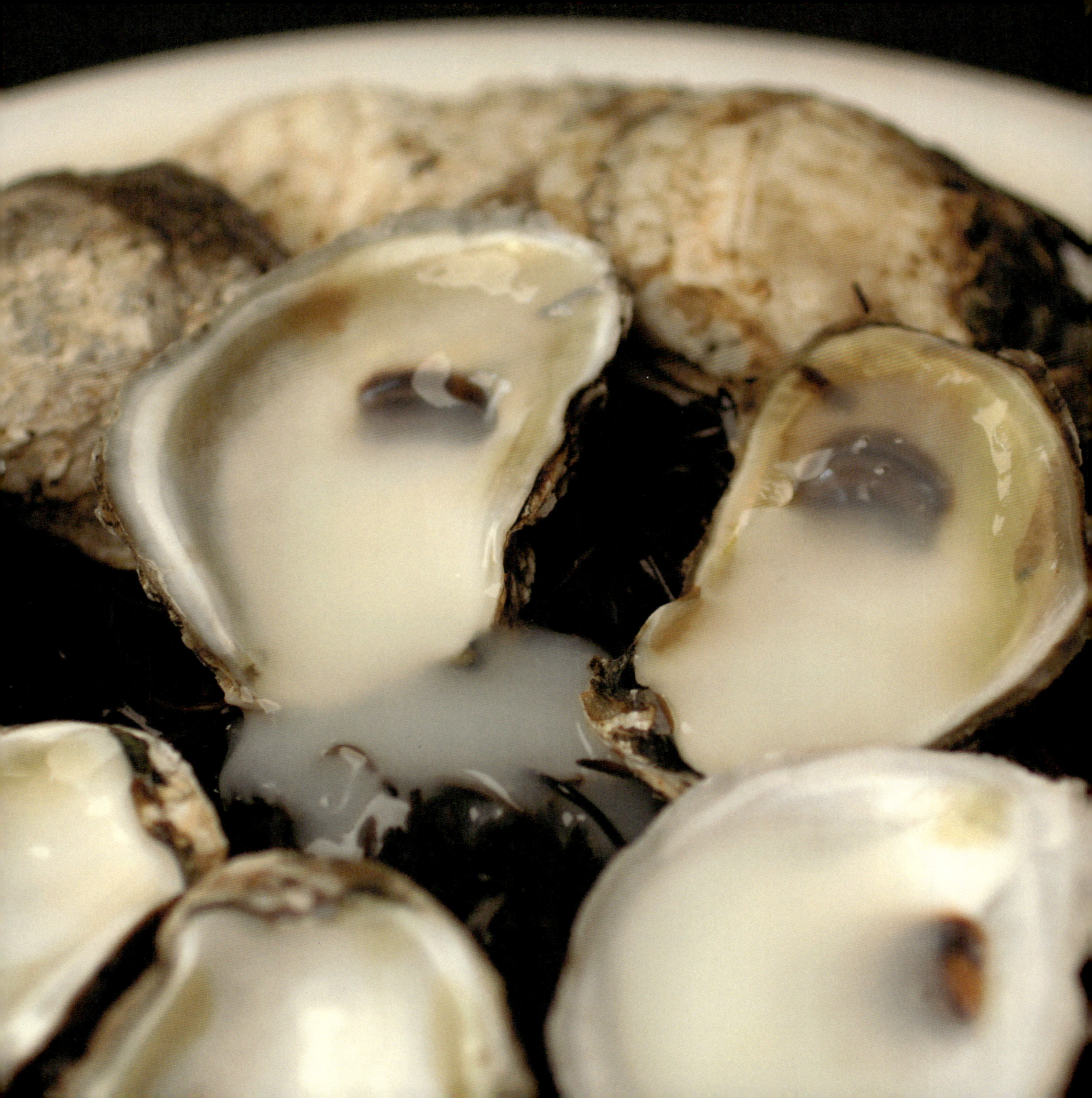

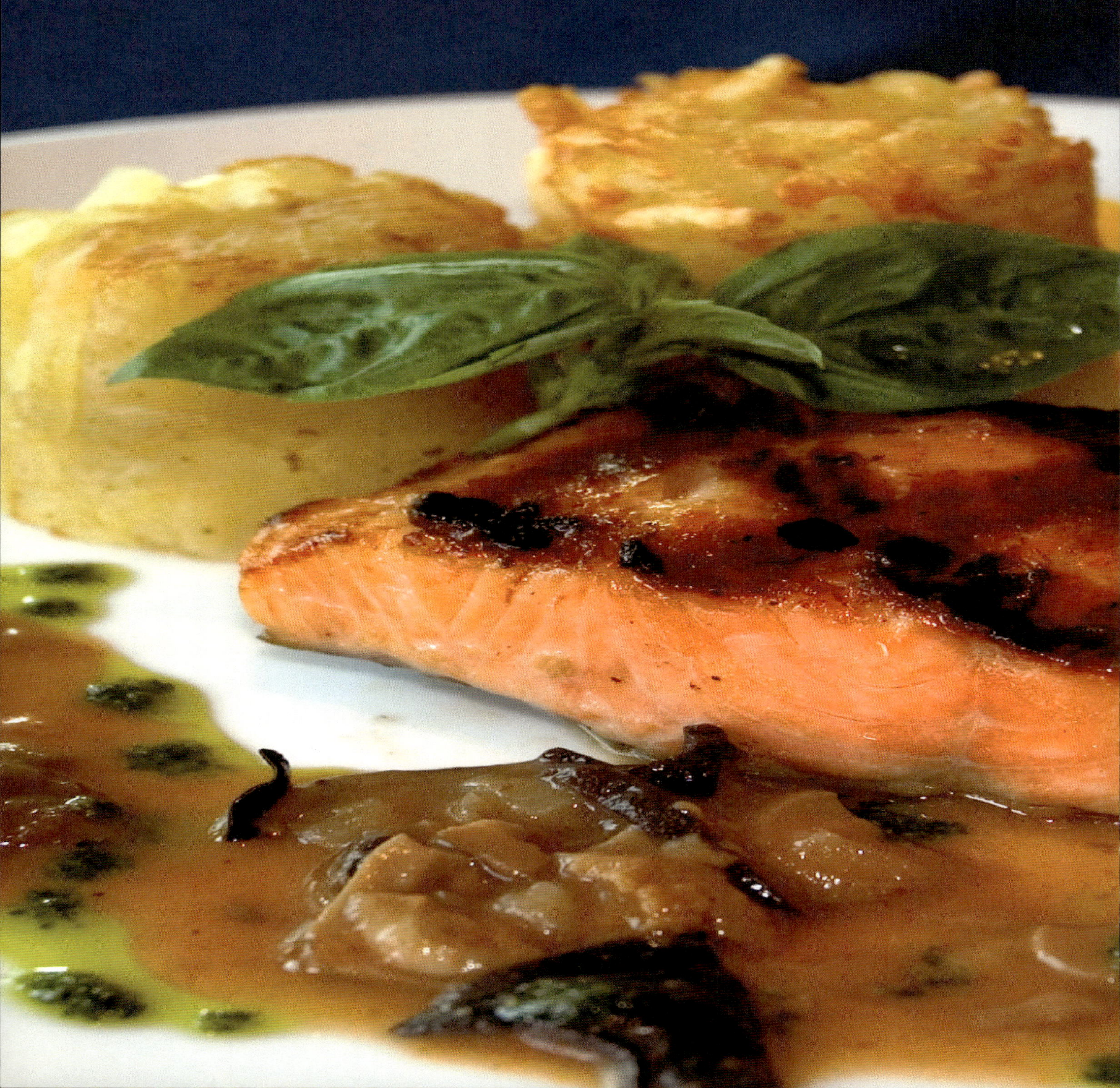

Grilled and glazed salmon

This recipe is just an example of how semen can be added to any of your favorite marinades.

Like chicken, salmon is very versatile, and can be marinated in a large variety of sauces to fit any occasion. Grilling the fish over coals adds a nice smokiness that compliments the distinct semen flavor. When adding semen to acidic marinades let it melt first before slowly stirring it in. Otherwise it may turn lumpy.

Glaze:

2-3 Tablespoons Honey

Tablespoon Lemon Juice

Tablespoons Soy Sauce

1 Teaspoon Mustard

1-2 Tablespoons Semen

1 Tablespoon Olive Oil

About 1 lb. Salmon Fillet

Mix all ingredients and marinade the fish in about half of the mixture for 20-30 minutes. Grill the salmon, preferable over coals, occasionally brushing the fish with the honey-sweet semen glaze.

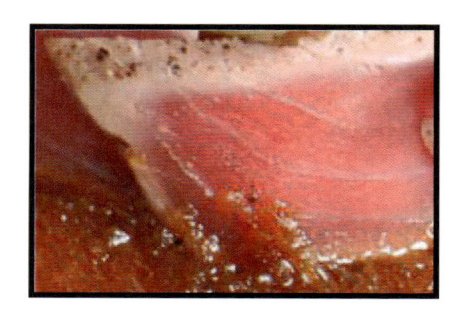

Tuna Sashimi with Dipping Sauce

Sashimi is raw fish served only with a dipping sauce. It is a good example of the subtlety in the Japanese kitchen. The delicate fish and the spicy sauce make a great appetizer. Fresh tuna and fresh semen are a splendid food combination.

Fresh Tuna

¼ Cup Soy Sauce

1/2 Cup Peanut Oil

2 Tablespoons Sesame Oil

1 Tablespoon Grated Garlic

1 Tablespoon Grated Ginger

1 Tablespoon Semen

Slice the tuna very thin and set aside. Whisk together remaining ingredients. Serve the tuna with the dipping sauce. Garnish with some simple greens and pickled ginger. For more semen flavor, omit the garlic and ginger.

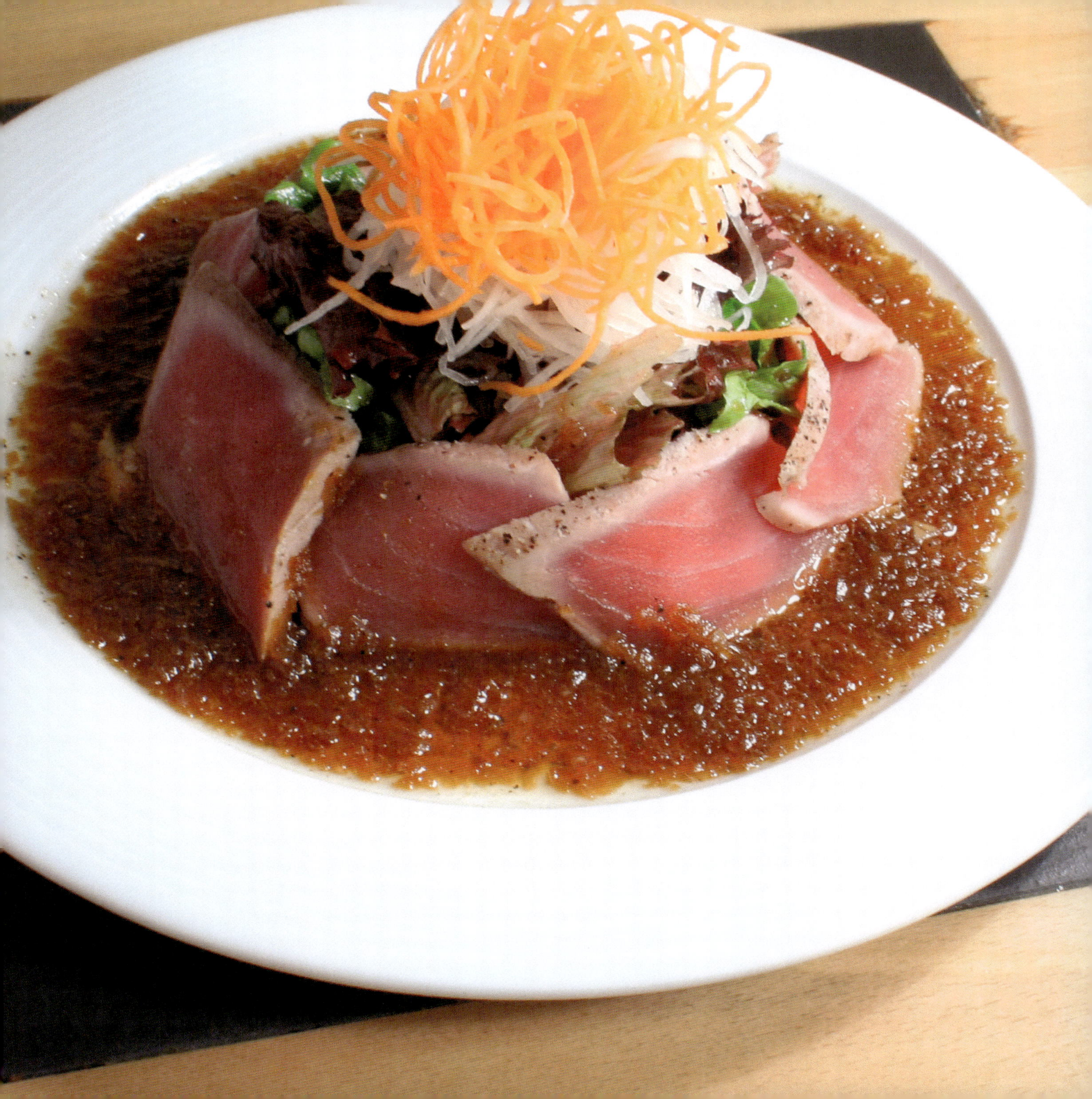

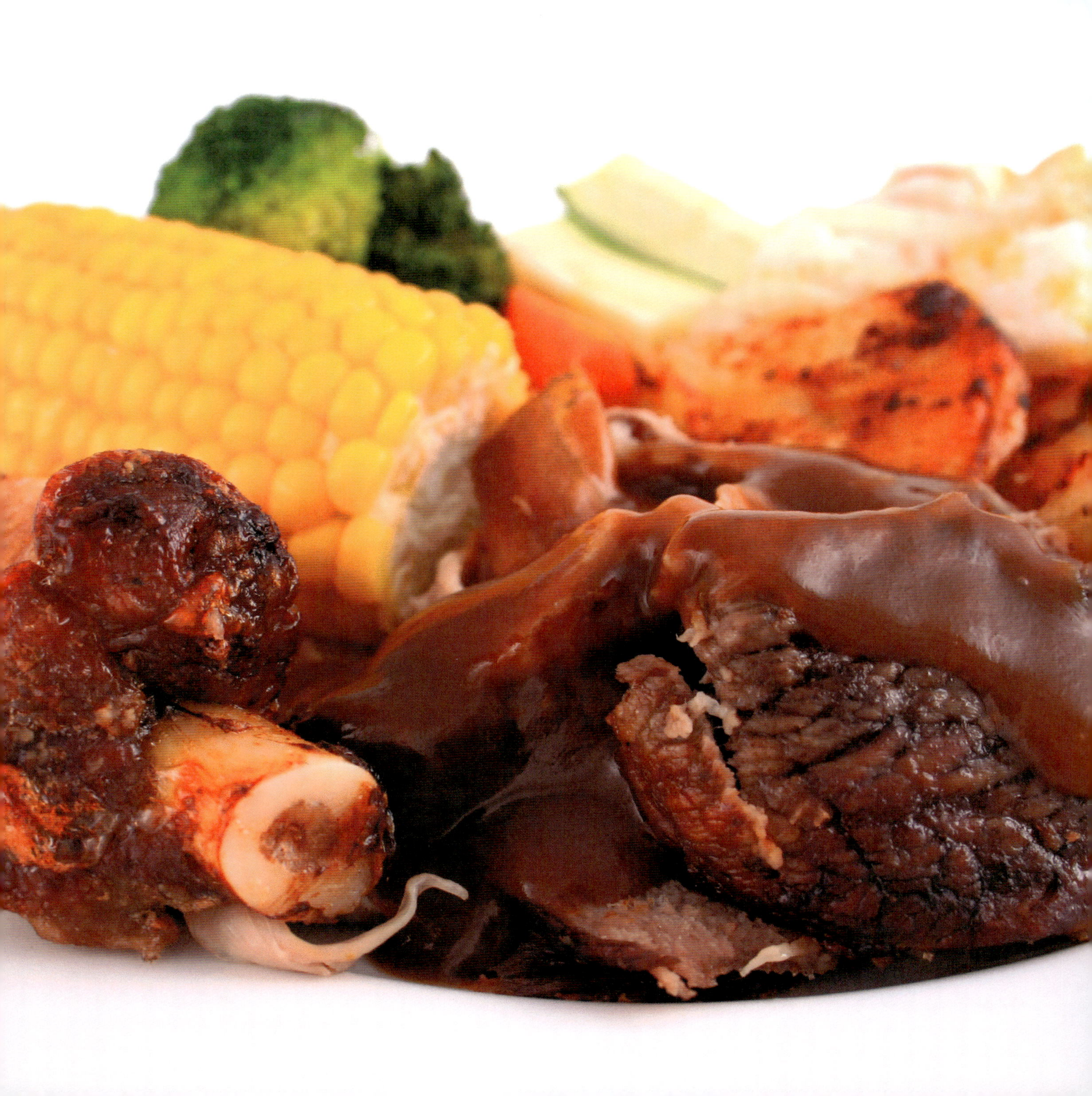

ROASTED LAMB WITH GOOD GRAVY

In many countries the traditional Sunday roast is the culinary and social highlight of the week. Cook the roast in your customary manner, and make this delicious gravy from the drippings.

2-3 Tablespoons of Fat and Drippings from the Roast

1 Tablespoon Flour

1-2 Tablespoons of Semen (Unheated)

1 Cup of Milk, Stock or Cream

Salt And Pepper

On medium heat stir the flour with a wire whisk into the drippings until thickened and smooth. Continue to cook slowly to brown the flour, and stir constantly. Slowly add the milk or stock and season with salt and pepper. Remove from heat and whisk in the semen. It is important that the gravy not be too hot since this stiffens the semen proteins and destroys the smooth texture.

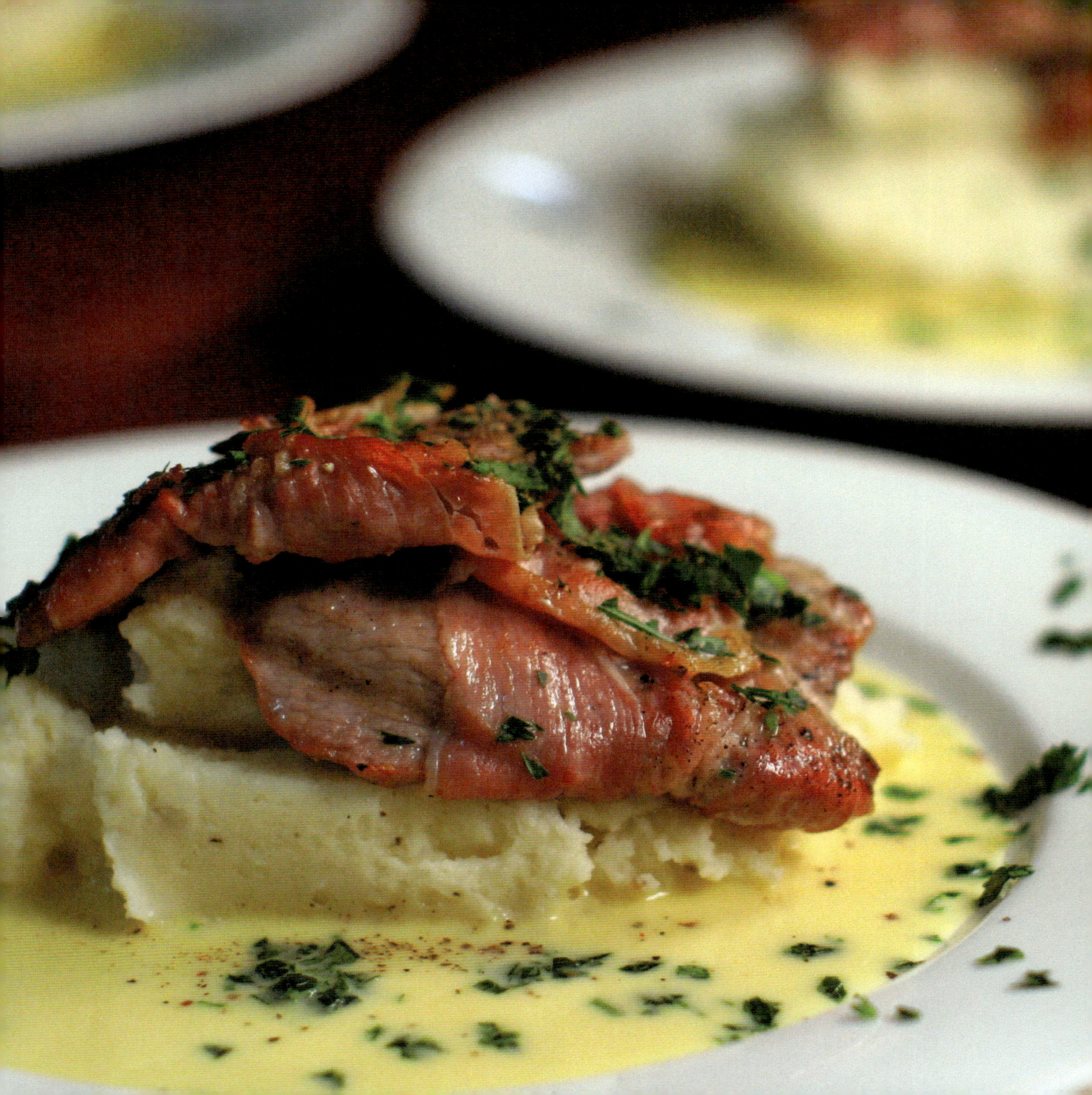

Veal scaloppini

The citrus and semen scaloppini sauce perfectly matches the delicate taste and texture of veal. In Italy the scaloppini sauce is poured over the meat immediately before serving – often right at the dinner table. For a luxurious Mediterranean touch serve the veal wrapped in Prosciutto with creamy mashed potatoes. If you have ample amounts of semen you can add it to the creamy mashed potatoes.

1 lb. Veal Escallops	2-3 Tablespoons Dry White Wine
3-4 Tablespoons Butter	Flour
Juice from One Lemon	Salt and White Pepper
1 Tablespoon Semen	Chopped Parsley

Start by pressing the lemon juice into the semen, it doesn't matter if it is lumpy since the mixture will be added to warm ingredients just before serving. Dust the veal with flour and sauté in butter for about 30 seconds on each side. Remove the meat and add more butter, when the butter gets hot add the wine. Quickly reduce the sauce and add the salt, pepper and parsley. Remove from heat and add the citrus semen. While very hot and foaming pour the sauce over the veal.

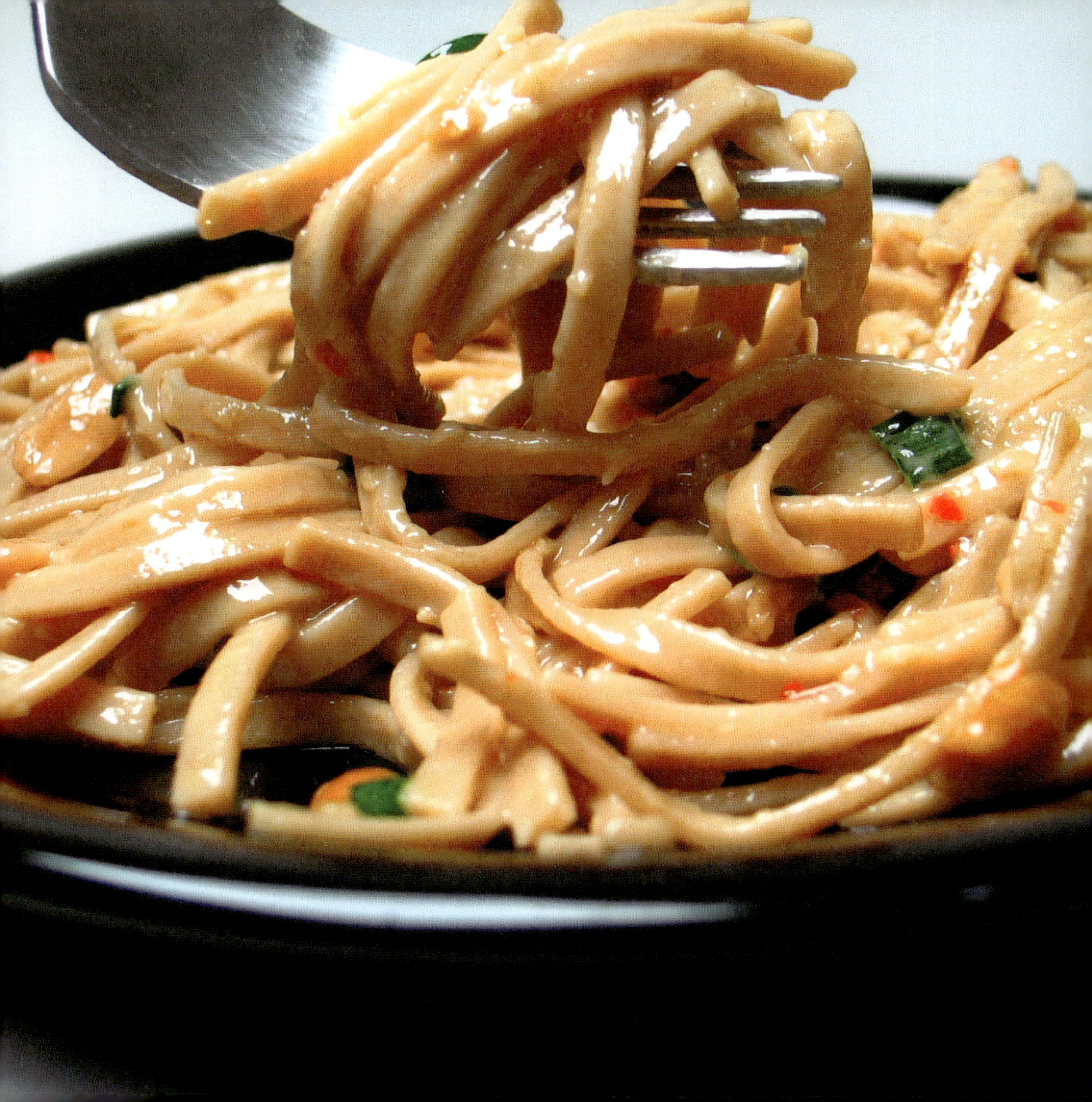

Noodles with special spicy sauce

The spicy ingredients in oriental cooking tend to dominate all other flavors, making it difficult to sense the delicate semen. This simple dish avoids that by striking a harmonious spicy-sweet-semen balance.

- 1 Package (2-4 Ounces) Of Noodles or Linguini
- 1 Tablespoon Soy Sauce
- 1-2 Tablespoons Sweet Chili Sauce
- ½ Cup Chicken or Vegetable Broth
- 1-2 Tablespoons of Semen
- 1 Clove Chopped Garlic
- 1 Tablespoon Chopped Ginger
- 1 Cup Assorted Fresh Vegetables Such As Broccoli, Leeks, Snap Beans Etc.
- 1/2 Tablespoon Oil

Boil the noodles or pasta and drain. Stir in the semen and sweet chili sauce into the warm (but not boiling) broth. Lightly fry the garlic and ginger in oil before adding the vegetables. Cook on high heat for about one minute before adding the semen broth mixture. Let it cook an additional 2-3 minutes. Serve immediately over the warm noodles.

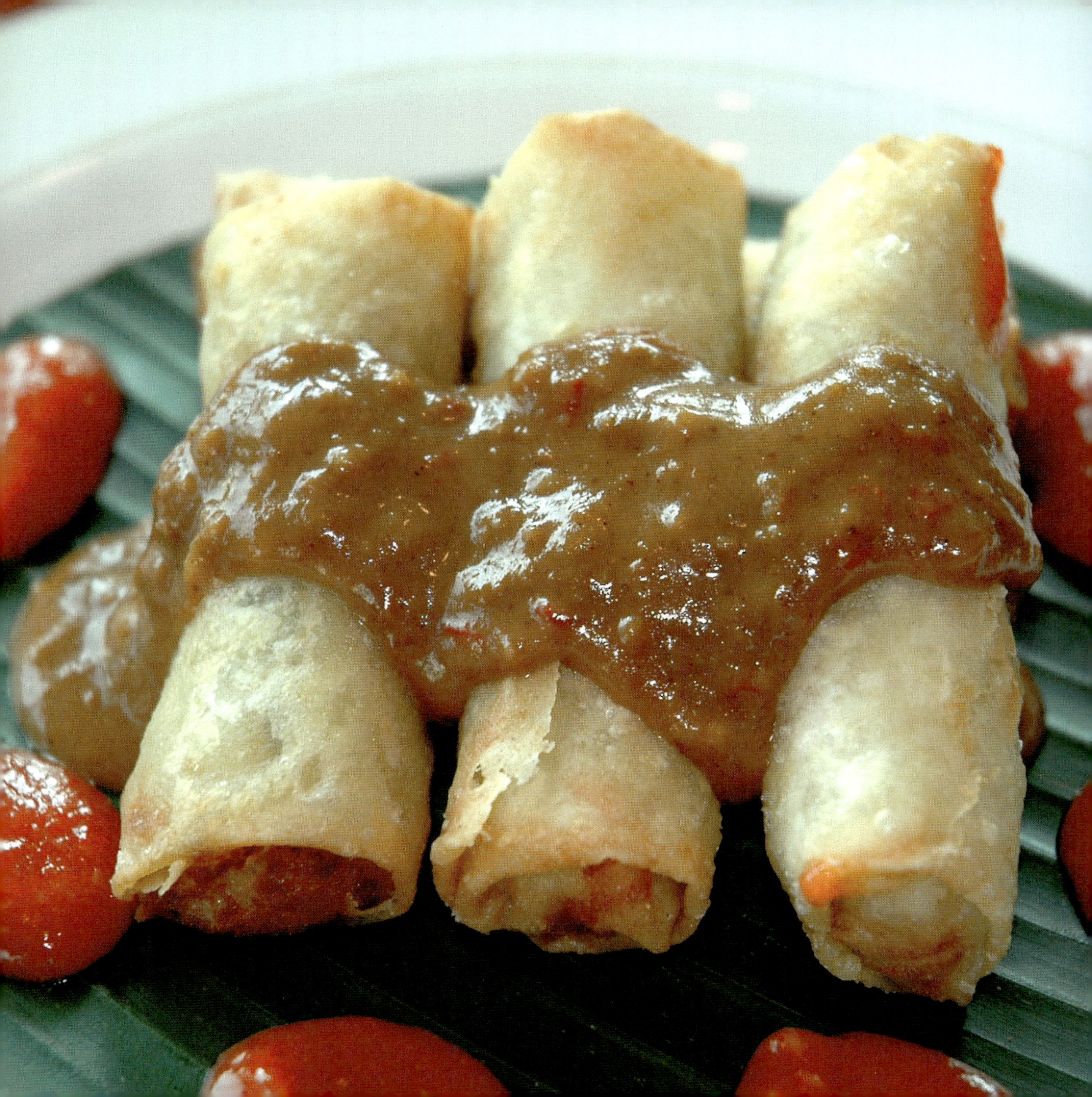

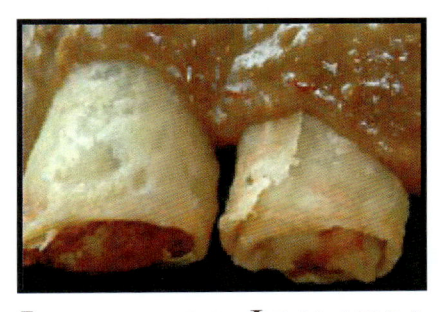

Lumpier Lumpia

Lumpia are spring rolls from the Philippines. This recipe is dedicated to a close Filipino friend who is dedicated to adding a semen spin to otherwise traditional dishes.

Filling:
1 Pound Ground Pork or Chopped Shrimp
1/4 Cup Chopped Water Chestnuts
1/2 Cup Finely Chopped Onions
1/4 Cup Minced Fresh Mushrooms
2 Egg Yolks
3 Teaspoons Soy Sauce
Salt And Pepper
Vegetable Oil
Fresh Spring Roll Wrappers

Sauce:
3 Cloves Minced Garlic
3 Tablespoons Brown Sugar
1 Tablespoon Semen
1/4 Cup Vinegar
Salt And Pepper To Taste

Mix all of the filling ingredients. Spoon a generous 1 teaspoon of filling on the each wrapper and roll them while folding in the sides and pinching them together as the filling rolls past them. Complete the roll by sealing the edges with water. Deep fry the rolls in oil until they turn a nice golden brown color. In a small saucepan, mix the vinegar, garlic, and brown sugar together over low heat. Remove from heat and add the semen, along with a little salt and pepper. Serve the rolls hot with warmed sauce.

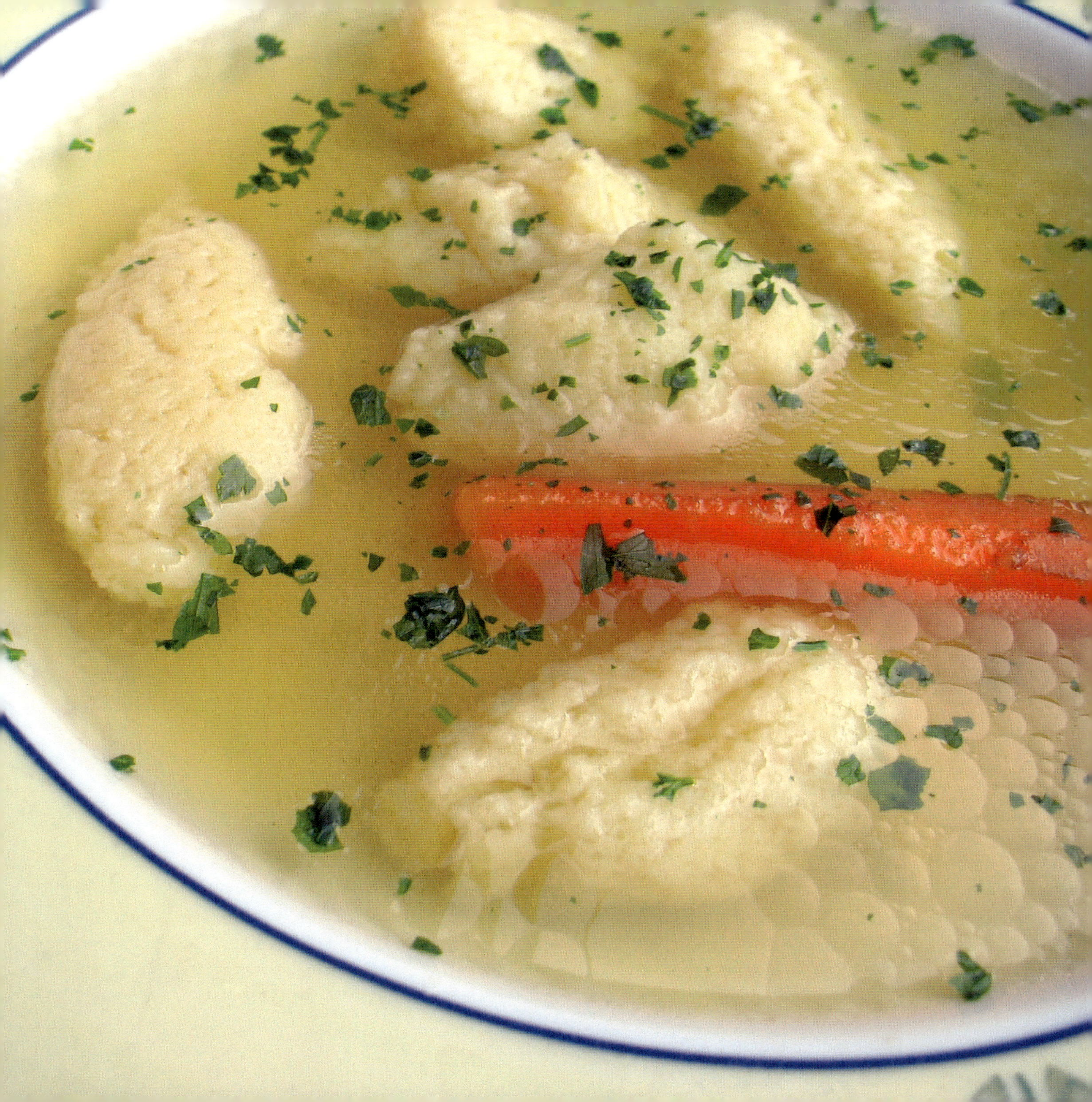

CHICKEN SOUP

Semen's versatile cooking properties allows us to add it to a clear broth soup with remarkable results. Chicken soup's healing properties will be made more potent by adding a healthy dose of fresh semen.

- 1 Chicken
- Cooked Noodles (Optional)
- Medium Sized Parsnip
- Carrots
- 1 Leek or Onion

- Stick of Celery
- Bay Leaves
- Tablespoons Semen
- Salt And Pepper
- Parsley for Garnishing

Cut the chicken and vegetables into appropriate pieces. Add everything to boiling water and let it slowly simmer for a couple hours or until the meat falls off the bones. Strain the broth and season with salt and pepper. Remove the meat from bones and add some of it to the clear broth; for color add a few cut carrots. For a heartier meal add some cooked noodles. For a clear broth add melted semen to slightly warm but not boiling broth while constantly stirring. If you prefer to see the semen in the soup quickly add fresh unmelted semen to boiling broth while gently stirring. The semen will then cook and turn into delicious thin velvety ribbons.

Special "S" BBQ Sauce

Masters of the barbecue pride themselves on their own special homemade BBQ sauce. The basic ingredients are well known but every cook adds a personal ingredient to give theirs a special flavor.

This is a basic recipe for a BBQ sauce, and the "S" is the special secret ingredient: Semen!

1 Cup Ketchup

3 Tablespoons Honey or Molasses

1 Tablespoon Lemon Juice

1 Tablespoon Semen

Dash of Hot Pepper Sauce

Combine the ingredients and brush on chicken or other meat during the final 10 minutes of grilling.

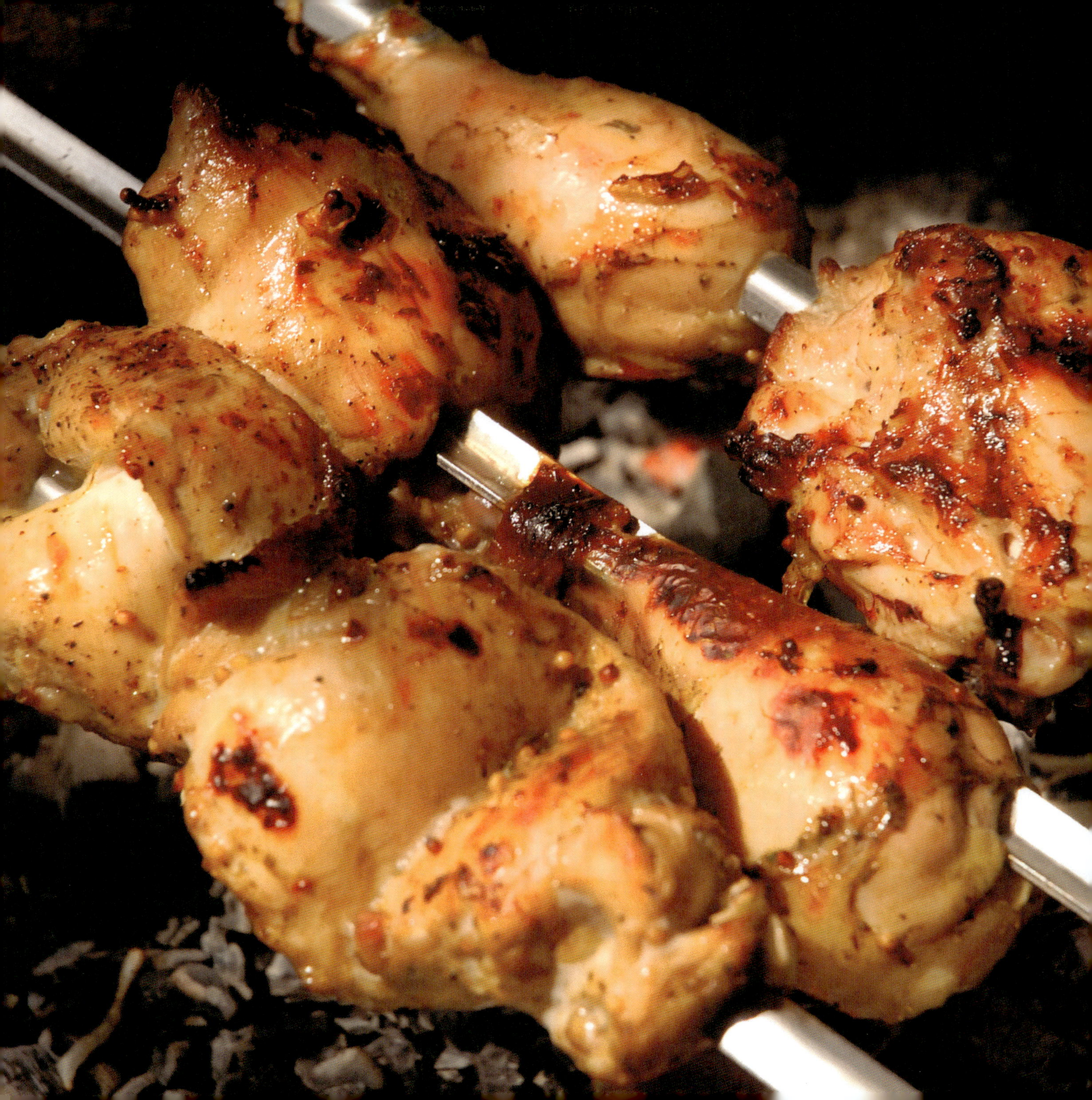

Hollandaise sauce

At first glance, this recipe seems easy - but this sauce may take a few trial-runs to get it right. The semen should be added along with the yolks in the beginning unless you are fond of semen lumps. The rich lemony sauce is a must for Eggs Benedict, but it is also delicious on steamed asparagus, or fish.

3 Egg Yolks
1/4 Cup Water
2 Tablespoons Lemon Juice
1/2 Cup Cold Butter
Fresh Semen
Dash of Salt and Pepper

In a small saucepan whisk together egg yolks, semen, water and lemon juice. Cook and stir over very low heat until mixture starts to slightly bubble. Cut the butter into several smaller chunks and add one piece at a time to the yolk mixture, whisking after each addition until melted and smooth. Stir in the salt and pepper. Serve immediately.

Chef's note: *It is possible to enhance the semen flavor by adding the semen drop by drop along with the butter. This does pose a risk of improper blending of the semen and a lumpy sauce.*

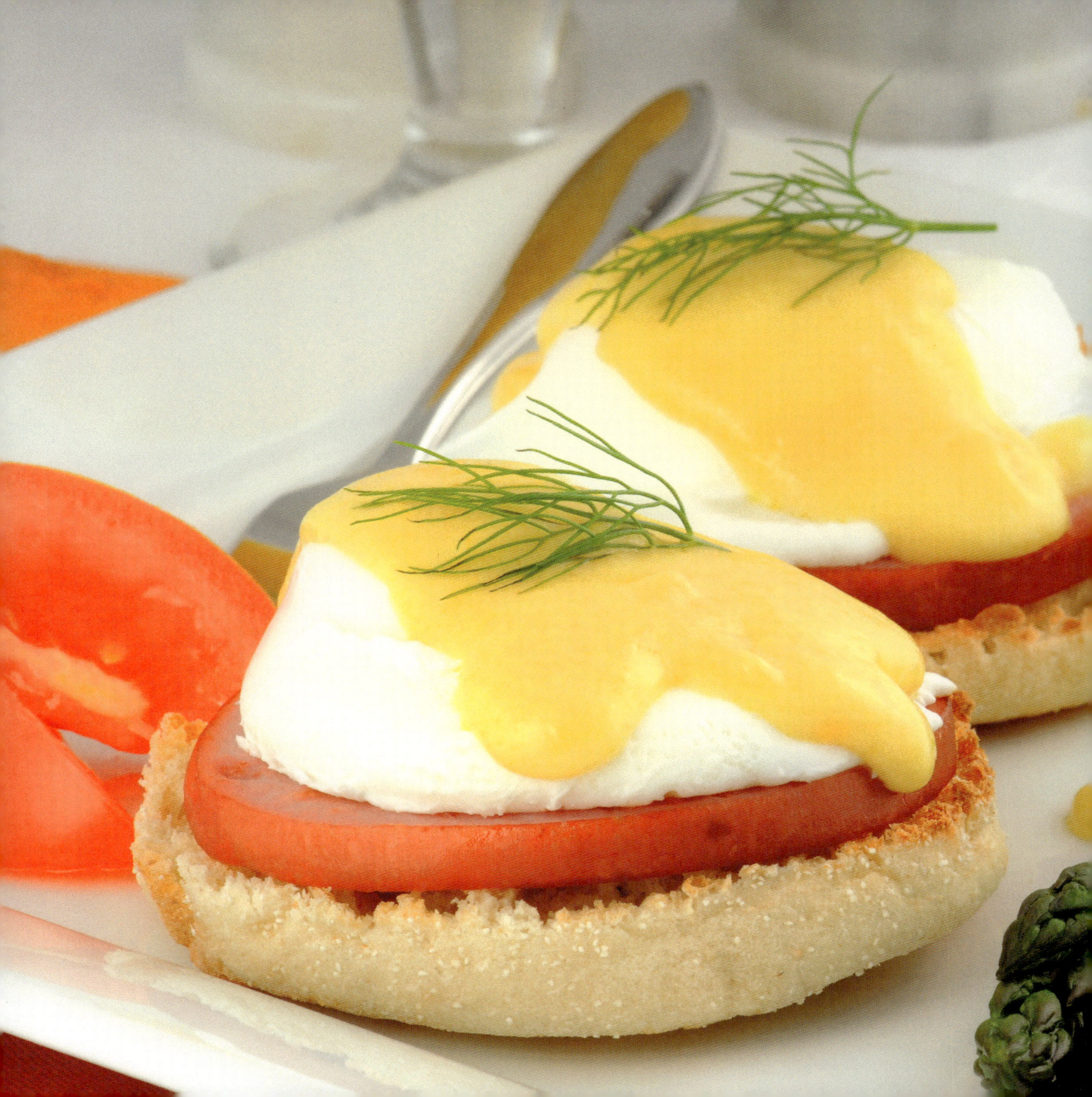

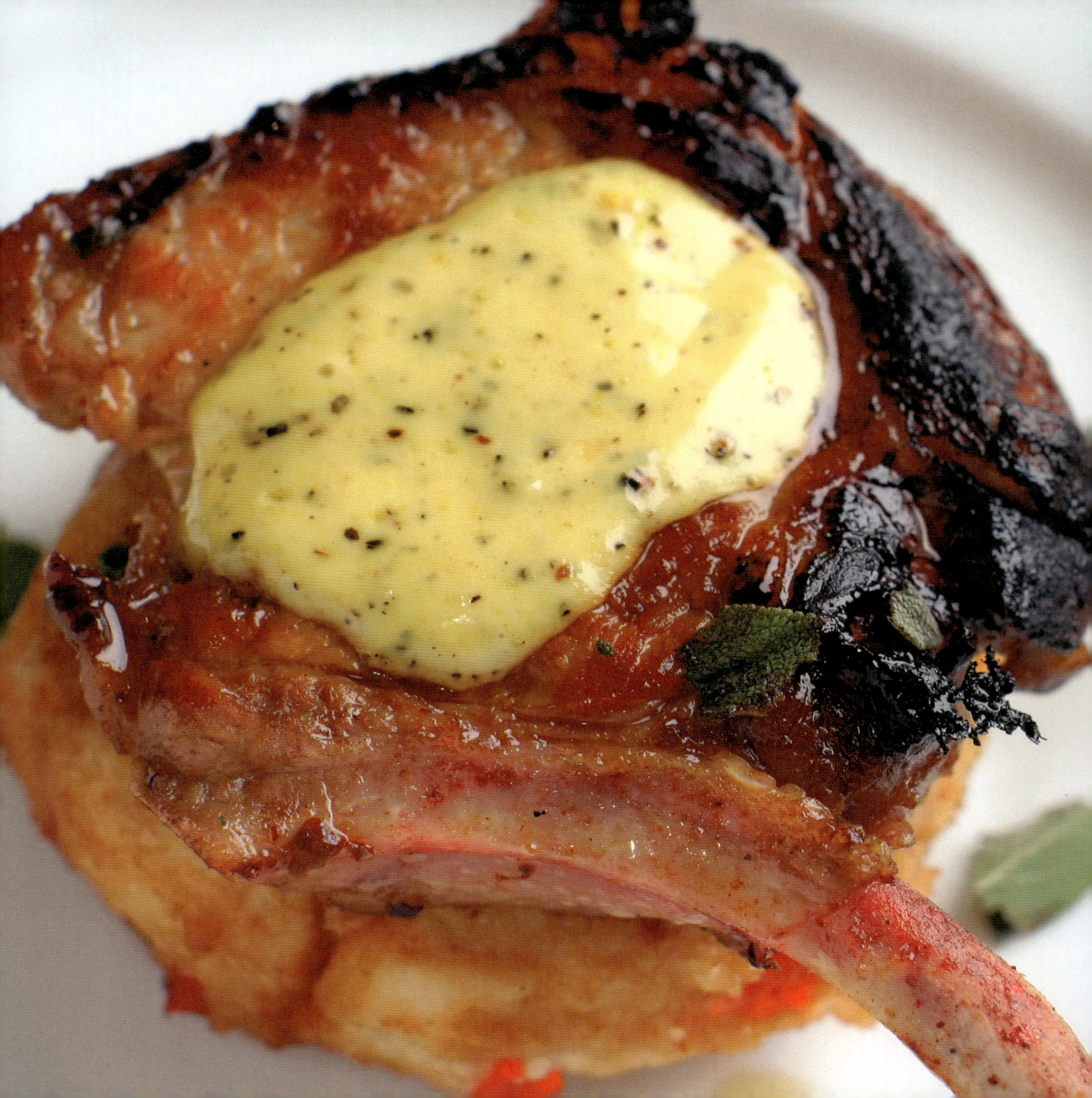

LIME AIOLI

Aioli is a wonderful sauce packed full of calories and smelly garlic. The lime gives the sauce a nice zesty kick and the semen flavor meshes nicely with the garlic and olive oil base. Don't try to hurry the procedure since it takes time and a lot of wrist action to absorb the oil into the egg.

1 Head Garlic

2 Egg Yolks

1-3 Tablespoons Fresh Semen

Pinch of Coarse Sea Salt

1 1/2 Cup of Quality Olive Oil

Juice from 1 Lime

1-2 Teaspoons Water

Start the preparation by making sure all ingredients are at room temperature. If you are using frozen semen, make sure that has thawed completely before beginning. Don't be afraid of using larger amounts of semen since this only intensifies the sauce's appeal. Crush the garlic along with the salt to obtain a smooth paste. Add the raw egg yolks and stir well. Slowly, drop by drop, add the olive oil to the paste, stirring constantly. When the mixture begins to thicken the oil can be added faster. When it gets thicker add the water and then mix in the remaining oil. Stir in first the lime first and then add the semen. For more semen flavor use less garlic.

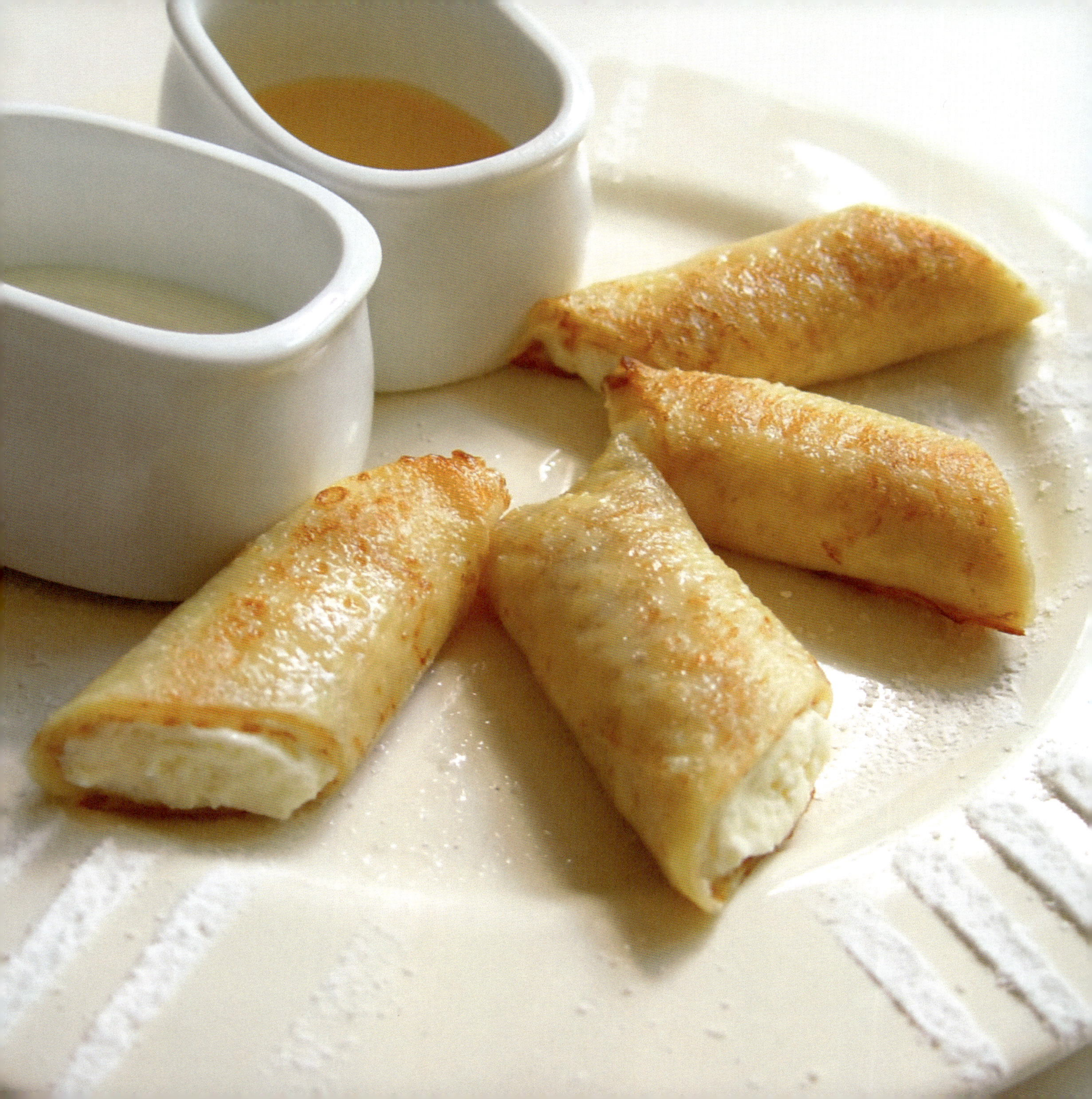

Creamy cum crêpes

Crepes are very versatile and can be served as a light snack, breakfast, or dessert, depending on the filling you choose. The subtle nuances of the semen in these crepes can be complimented by a dry cider.

Crepes:

3 Eggs

1 Cup Flour

1 Cup Milk

1/2 Teaspoon Salt

2 Tablespoons Melted Butter

Filling:

1/2 Cup Cottage Cheese

2 Tablespoons Semen

1/3 Cup Melted Butter

1/4 Cup Powdered Sugar

Blend all ingredients for the crepes until smooth. Melt a small piece of butter in a hot skillet. Pour a small amount of batter on the pan while swirling it to distribute the batter evenly and make a thin crepe. Let it cook a few seconds until golden brown and then cook the other side.

Whisk together the powdered sugar and melted butter. Fold in the cottage cheese and semen. Spoon the filling into the crepes and serve right away.

Cum crème caramel

Semen adds a titillating touch to this French classic. It is sure to impress any dinner guest.

Custard:

1 Cup Sugar

3 Tablespoons Water

1 1/2 Cups Whipping Cream

1/2 Cup Milk

1 Tablespoon Fresh Semen

3 Large Egg Yolks

1 Large Egg

Chocolate Sauce:

1 Cup Semisweet Chocolate

3/4 Cup Whipping Cream

1 Teaspoon Vanilla

1. Add 2/3 cup of sugar and water to saucepan and place over low heat. Stir until the sugar dissolves, then increase the heat to a gentle boil. Boil until the mixture turns deep golden brown. Pour caramel mixture into ramekins and coat bottoms thoroughly.

2. Bring cream, milk and remaining sugar to a boil until the sugar dissolves. Whisk in fresh semen, yolks and egg. Pour the custard mixture into caramel-lined ramekins. Place the ramekins in a baking pan and add hot water until it reaches halfway up the sides of the ramekins. Bake about 30 minutes at 375 degrees Fahrenheit, then remove and chill.

3. In a small saucepan over low heat, heat chocolate and whipping cream, stirring until chocolate is melted and sauce is smooth. Stir in vanilla.

4. Invert the crème caramels onto plates and top with a slightly warmed chocolate sauce.

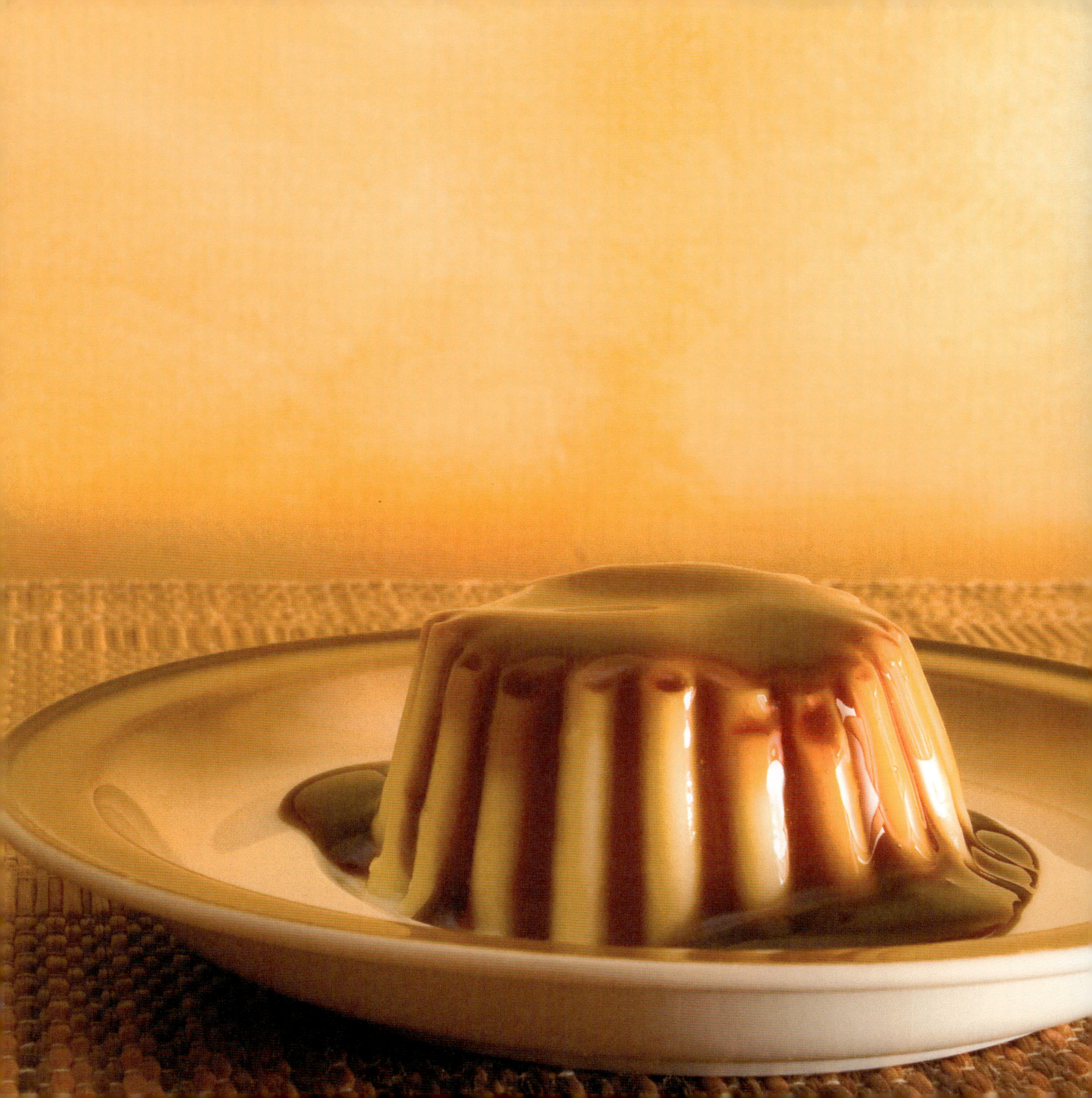

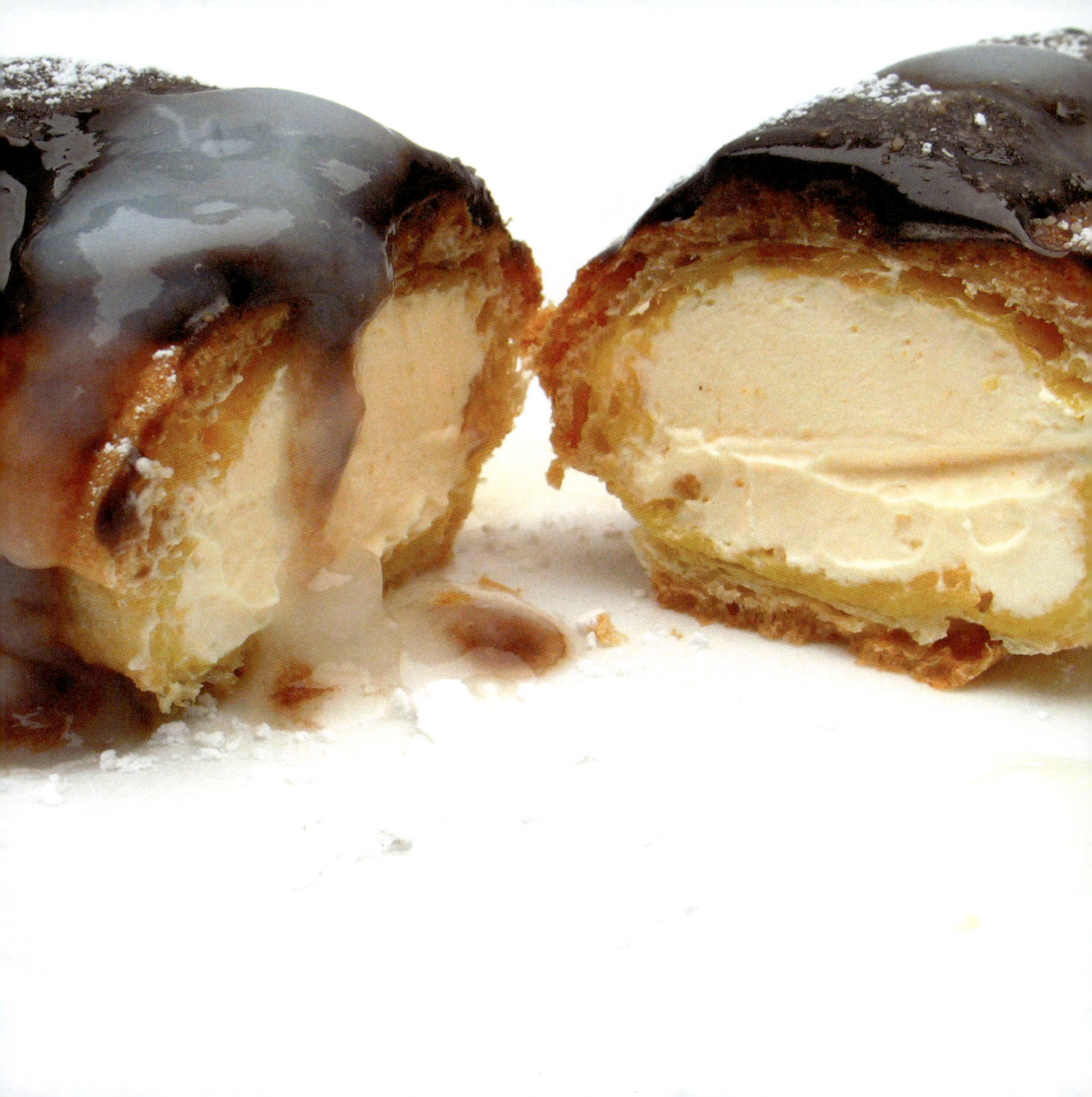

Chocolate cream éclair

Making the pastry dough called 'pate a choux' is not as difficult as it seems at first.
If you give it a try you will be greatly rewarded.

1/2 Cup Flour

1/2 Teaspoon Sugar

1/4 Teaspoon Salt

1/4 Cup Butter

1/2 Cup Water

2 Large Eggs

Stiffly Whipped Cream

Semen

Mix the flour, sugar and salt in a bowl and bring the water to a boil in a heavy saucepan over medium heat and add the butter. Remove the saucepan from the heat and quickly stir in the flour mixture. Return to heat and stir constantly until the dough lets go of the sides of the pan and forms a thick smooth ball. Remove from heat again and let the dough cool a little. Add the first egg while continuously stirring. Once the dough is smooth add the second egg and stir until smooth. Spoon small finger shaped mounds of dough onto the baking sheet a couple of inches apart and bake at 400 degrees for 15 minutes. Then reduce the oven temperature to 350 degrees and bake for a further 30 to 40 minutes until the shells are a nice amber color.

Add semen to heavy cream and whip stiff. Split the pastry and fill with whipped semen cream. If you have a lot of semen available you can garnish the éclairs with a simple glaze of powdered sugar and semen. Dust with powdered sugar.

SPUNKY CANDIED PECANS

This is a great party snack. Prepare well in advance and let guests enjoy your delicious nuts while you put the finishing touch on their dinner. Pecans are the best but other nuts can also be used.

½ Cup Sugar

3 Cups Pecans or Other Savory Nuts

3 Tablespoons Melted Butter

1-2 Tablespoons Fresh Semen

Toss the pecans gently in the melted butter on large baking sheet and bake at 350 degrees several minutes until the nuts are lightly browned. Combine the sugar and semen and perhaps a little more butter in a small bowl before stirring into the pecans. Bake another 5-8 minutes until the sugar hardens.

Let cool before serving.

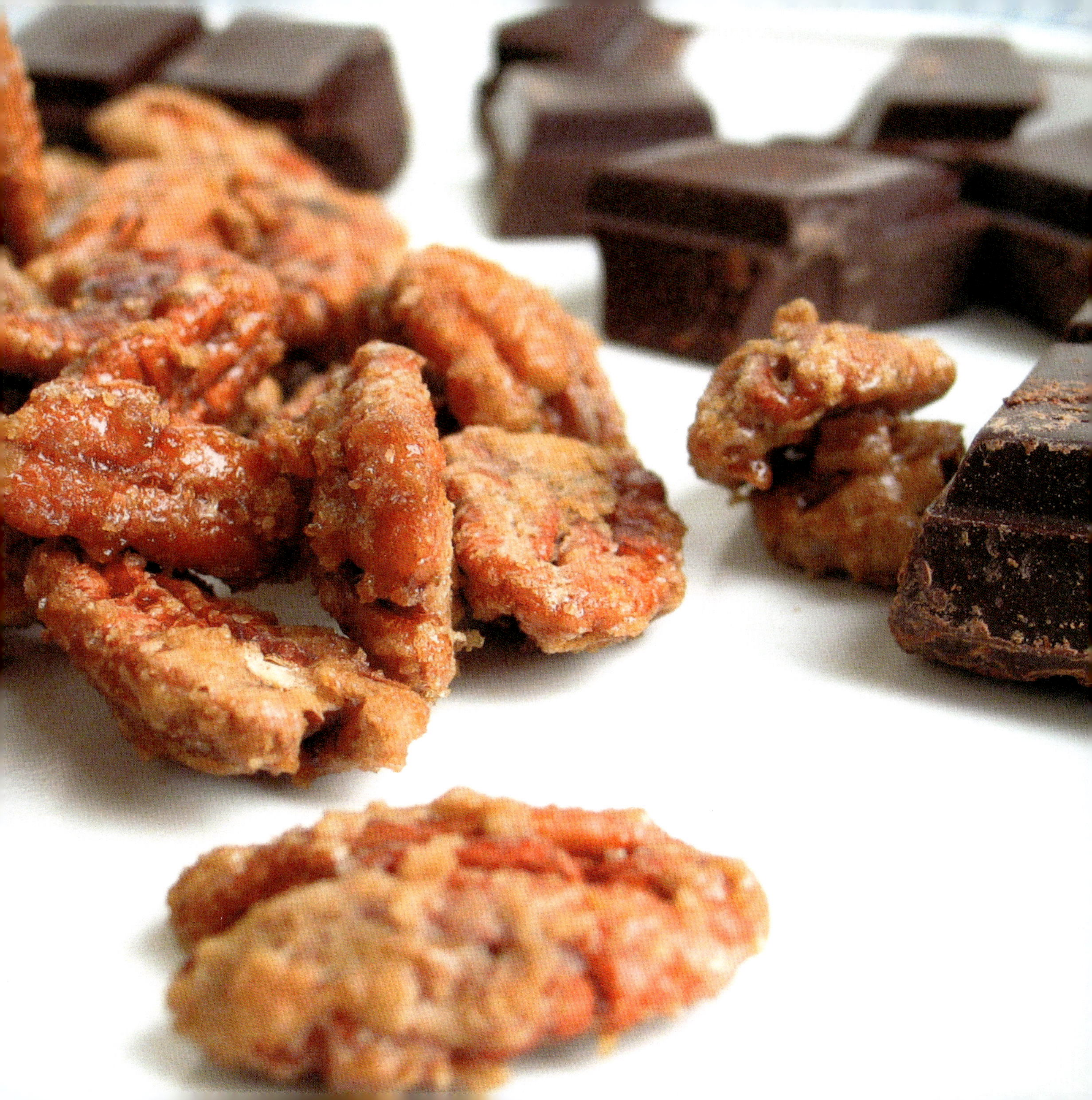

Creamy dessert
Panna Cotta

Panna Cotta means "cooked cream" in Italian. It is a creamy dessert made of cream, semen, sugar, and vanilla. It only takes minutes to make and can easily be prepared in advanced.

- ½ Teaspoon Unflavored Gelatin
- 1/4 Cup Milk
- 1/4 Cups Whipping Cream

- 1-3 Tablespoons Semen
- 1/2 Cup Sugar
- 1/2 Teaspoon Pure Vanilla Extract

Place the gelatin in the milk let this mixture sit for about 5 minutes. Combine the cream and sugar in a saucepan and bring it to a boil, stirring to dissolve the sugar. Once the cream is hot, remove the saucepan from the heat and stir in the gelatin mixture, semen and vanilla. Stir until the gelatin has completely dissolved. Pour the cream into small glasses or cups place in the refrigerator to chill for 2 - 4 hours until set.

Chef's note: Increase the amount of gelatin in this recipe when using larger quantities of semen.

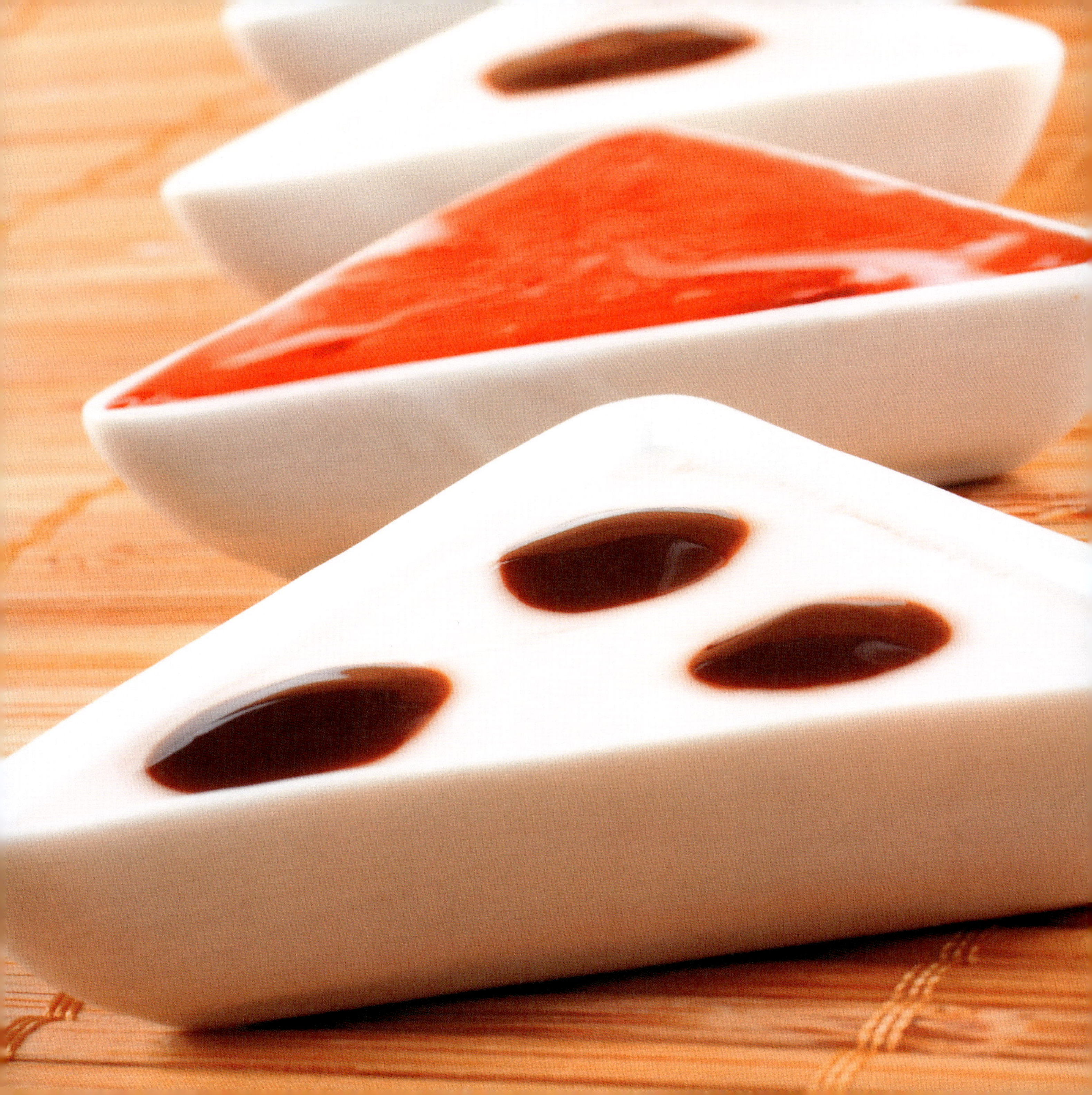

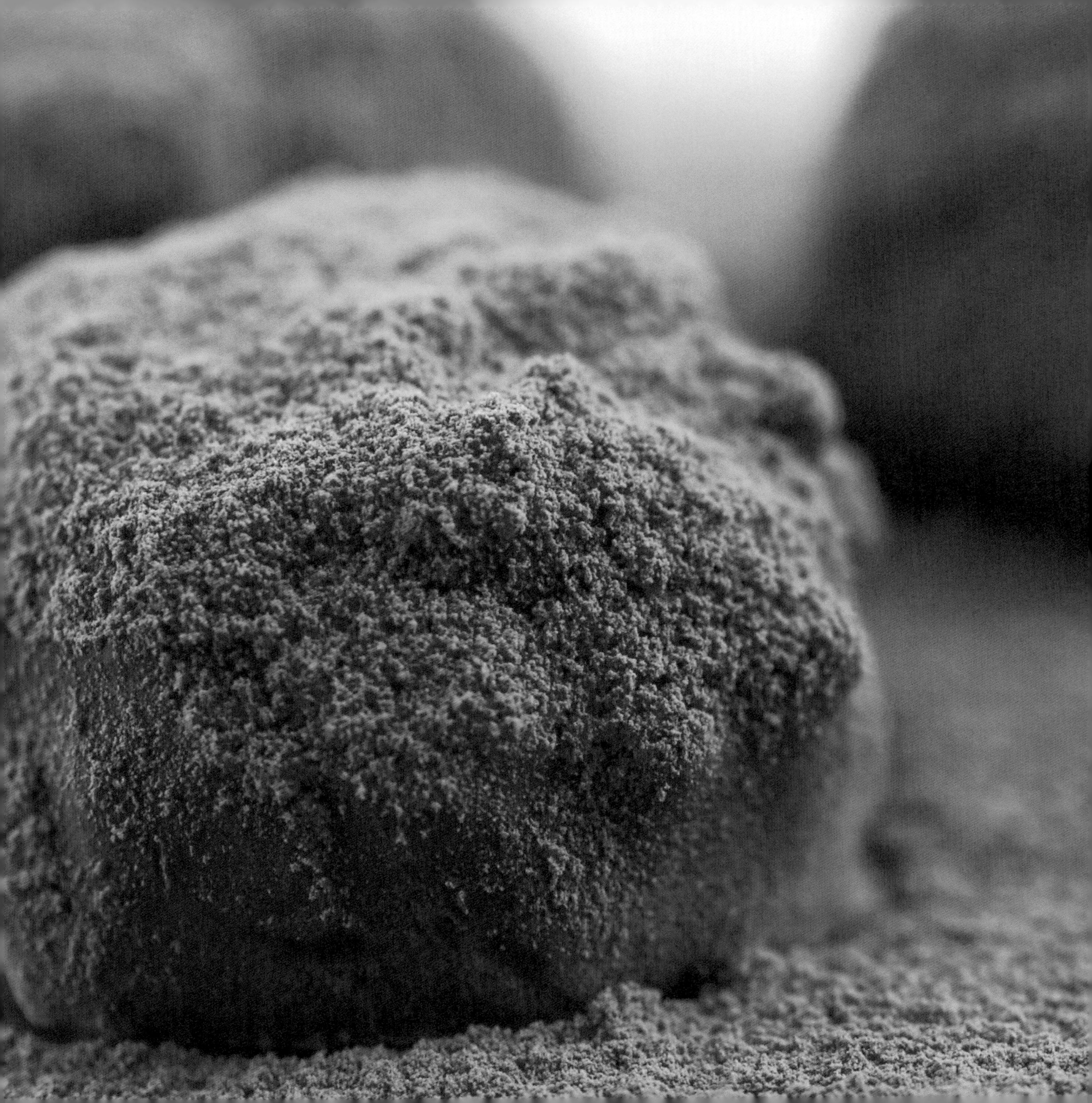

Chocolate truffles with white creamy center

These semen-filled chocolate truffles are a definite favorite! The dark chocolate truffle is filled with a smooth white semen flavored ganache. Only use the highest quality chocolate in order to guarantee satisfaction.

Ganache:

1 Generous Cup of White Chocolate

1 Cup of Whipping Cream

1 Tablespoon Semen

½ Teaspoon Pure Vanilla Extract (Optional)

Coating:

1 Cup of Dark Chocolate

3/4 Cup Cocoa

Chop the chocolate into the thinnest slivers possible. Heat the cream in the microwave but do not let it boil. Pour just enough of the hot cream to cover the chopped white chocolate. Wait a few seconds and stir carefully until smooth. Keep stirring and slowly add the rest of the cream, finally adding the vanilla and semen, stirring until smooth.

Chill the ganache, then roll it into small balls and place on a baking sheet. Chill the ganache again while you carefully melt the dark chocolate. Using a fork, dip the balls of white semen ganache into the melted dark chocolate. Repeat the coating procedure, then dust with cocoa.

Tiramisu

Tiramisu is a rich dessert with layers of ladyfinger cookies soaked in a semen-espresso-cognac concoction with an airy mascarpone and cream filling.

- 8 Ladyfinger Cookies 1/2 Cup Espresso
- 2 Teaspoons Sugar
- 2 Tablespoons Cognac
- 1-2 Tablespoons Fresh Semen

- 1/2 Cup Whipping Cream
- 1/2 Cup Mascarpone Cheese
- 2 Tablespoons Sugar
- 1 Teaspoon Pure Vanilla Extract

Place a layer of ladyfingers on the bottom of the pan and let them fully absorb the mixture of semen, sugar, espresso and brandy. Layer the soaked cakes with the mascarpone cream mixture, either in a pan or in individual glasses. Garnish with shaved chocolate. This dessert actually gets better if it is made a day in advanced.

Chef's note: A great variation is to use the semen in the cream instead soaking the ladyfingers in it.

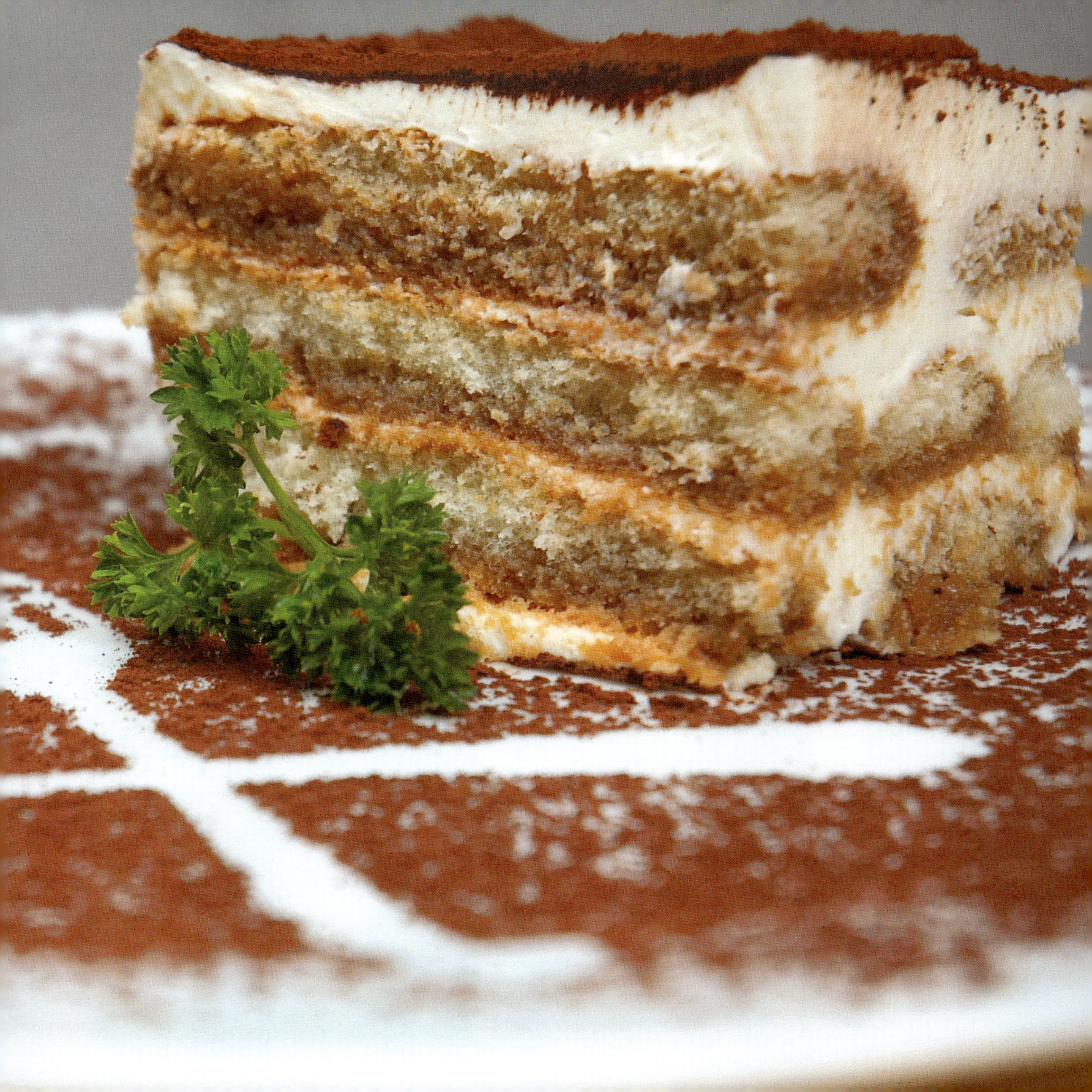

Nutritional Information

Semen is nutritious. It contains a good balance of fructose sugars, protein, enzymes, vitamins and minerals. On its own, semen meets the criteria for a low-carb food. In fact, Dr. Atkins would probably have praised semen as an ideal food had it not been considered a faux pas.

Like any other natural organic product, the quality of semen depends on the health of its producer. Generally, healthy males produce high quality semen and vice-versa. As long as the semen is fresh and properly harvested, there is little risk of contamination. The quality and quantity of sperm is irrelevant when semen is eaten, so even vasectomized males can produce semen that is wonderful for cooking. The important factors are flavor, volume, and consistency.

Semen ingredients: Fructose, sorbitol, inositol, glutathione, deoxyribonucleic acid, creatine, phosphorus, zinc, magnesium, calcium, potassium, ascorbic acid, vitamin B12, choline, testosterone, prostagladins, lactic acid, uric acid, nitrogen

Flavor

The words used to describe the flavors and aromas associated with semen vary dramatically from person to person. Some tend to dismiss semen as food and describe it as bitter or salty. This is similar to a person who tastes wine for the first time says that wine tastes sour. Like all other foods, the tastes and aromas of semen open up and are better appreciated when you are able to compare and discuss the different tastes with other connoisseurs. Semen is a complex food and has numerous different olfactory nuances. Some common associations are: Brie cheese, cookie dough, almond, salty, spicy, sweet, bitter, yeast, alfalfa sprouts, fishy, cocoa, and fruity.

There are many different foods and supplements that may improve the flavor of semen. Fresh fruit or fruit juices seem to have a positive effect on semen taste; pineapple, citrus fruits, mango, cranberry and grape juice are most preferable. Some sources recommend parsley, wheatgrass, fresh mint, and even celery to improve semen flavor. Strong or peculiar tasting foods like asparagus, garlic, Brussels sprouts, broccoli, cabbage, and spicy foods will also infuse semen with a distinct flavor.

In order to fully enjoy the wonderful taste of natural unadulterated semen I strongly recommend that you not intentionally attempt to alter the taste of the semen used in cooking. However once you have gained some experience of cooking with semen feel free to be more adventurous and begin experimenting with purposely taste altered semen.

Chef's note: *While testing the recipes for this book the chefs discovered that eating raw ginger and drinking large quantities of ginger tea gave their semen a pleasant exotic flavor.*

Volume and texture

The average ejaculation is about a teaspoon or two of semen, and this is usually not enough semen when it is used for cooking purposes. So volume enhancing methods are important when semen is used gastronomically. There are two main methods to enhance semen volume. The surest way is to collect semen after a restful night's sleep since this is when semen volume is at its peak. Another method is ex- tended foreplay. While writing this cookbook, the authors found that extended genital stimulation will almost always increase the amount of semen ejaculated. Texture on the other hand is not a factor that is very controllable; but making sure that the semen producer remains properly hydrated is the key to both high volume and consistent texture.

Chef's note: *Plan your semen dinner in advance by collecting semen in the morning and then again just before it is called for in the recipe. That way you will probably have enough for most of the recipes in this book. Just remember to refrigerate the semen to keep it fresh*

Cooking properties

The cooking properties of semen are similar to egg whites, with the only real difference being the volumes used. Since semen is usually only available in smaller amounts, most of the recipes utilize semen for its taste, and only secondly for its smooth texture or nutrition. Most of the recipes instruct that the semen be added towards the end of the cooking process or in the final stages of making a sauce. This is so that the delicate flavors do not risk getting overwhelmed by the other ingredients or destroyed by the cooking process.

When freshly ejaculated, semen usually has a thick lumpy consistency. Left untouched it will then "melt" and turn more fluid. Some semen cooks prefer using semen in its melted state while others enjoy ejaculating directly into the sauce pan or mixing bowl. The recipes in this book sometimes specify "melted" semen but using "unmelted" will not affect the taste of the final food dish.

Chef's note: Heat up a lightly oiled frying pan/skillet. Remove from heat and ejaculate directly into the pan, return to heat and fry the semen without stirring. This will create a mini-omelette, or in some cases, many small omelette-drops. Salt and pepper to taste. This is the perfect introductory recipe for newbie semen cookers.

Storing semen

Fresh semen should be eaten or cooked within a few hours since the taste quickly deteriorates. Once chilled, semen can be stored for up to three days in the fridge. If you don't plan on using it within three days I recommend that you freeze it. Frozen semen should always be thawed slowly at room temperature or in the fridge in order to minimize deterioration.

Chef's note: *Keep a small container in the freezer and simply add (ejaculate) into the container every morning and then return it to the freezer. This way you will always have sufficient amounts of semen for cooking. By saving semen in this manner, you can quickly begin experimenting with the recipes that require larger quantities. Also, the frozen semen can be mixed with syrup and shaved ice to make yummy ice cones.*

Printed in Great Britain
by Amazon